More Than Physical: *A Collector's Guide*

By Gregory Branson–Trent

Published by Collector's Guide Publishing, Box 62034, Burlington, Ontario, Canada, L7R 4K2
Editor - Carl Krach

Manufactured in Canada
Olivia – More Than Physical: A Collector's Guide / Gregory Branson–Trent
First Edition
ISBN 0-9695736-6-9

This book is lovingly dedicated to the woman who inspired it.
Thank you Olivia, for the music and entertainment.

Also for Mark, Benita, Jeri, Matt, Mary, and my parents.

Olivia Newton-John is one of the most recognized and popular artists of our time. She has continually proven herself to be the greatest female artist in history. She has conquered every market available to a musician and an actress. Along with countless awards and recognitions, she has maintained a successful career for more than twenty years.

Her style ranges from sweet and soft to hot and rough. She's taken us from country, to easy listening, to pop, and never stopped giving us great music along the way. With number one records like "Have You Never Been Mellow," "I Honestly Love You," "Magic," "Physical," and "You're The One That I Want," she conquered *Billboard*'s music charts.

I became fascinated with her in the early '70s when "Let Me Be There" was released. I stayed with her through "If You Love Me (Let Me Know)" all the way to her latest single "No Matter What You Do." I've followed her through every facet of her career—from the queen of mellow, to film queen, to queen of kink in the '80s—every new move in her career so strategically planned to carry her to the title "superstar."

When I began writing my first book, I couldn't think of anyone I'd rather write about. My fascination grows with every release, and I hope yours will too with this collection. The contents of this book will take you through her entire career and give you a good mix of a career that's lasted over two decades.

—*Gregory Branson-Trent*

Promotional picture released by MCA Records

Contents

Promotional picture released by MCA Records

INTRODUCTION

When Olivia Newton-John burst onto the scene as a guest on Cliff Richard's BBC-TV series, few realized the impact this wide-eyed girl from Down Under would have. In a little over two decades, she would become nothing short of a superstar. Olivia is the girl Cliff Richard chose to sing with him on his first duet record. She is also the girl Harry Saltzman chose for the starring part in the movie, *Toomorrow*.

Since her early years, Olivia has grown and gone through a variety of stages: singer, songwriter, author, actress, entrepreneur, and environmentalist, to name a few. She's hit the top of the charts with such hits as "Physical," "Have You Never Been Mellow," "I Honestly Love You," "Magic," and "You're The One That I Want"; she's starred in the films *Grease*, *Xanadu*, *Two Of A Kind*, and *A Mom For Christmas;* she's released an unusually large group of music videos; she received a Grammy for the video "Physical"; and she's also had a number of hit television specials. In other words, she's multi-talented.

Olivia burst onto the scene as the girl-next-door in the early 1970s, but by the latter part of the decade, her music took on a more vampy sound. Titles such as "You're The One That I Want," "Totally Hot," "Physical," "Soul Kiss," and "I Need Love" created a new image and showed us where Olivia Newton-John could take us. Today, she's headed into a new era, with music she's written herself. She's determined to make the kind of music she wants to, even if it's not aimed at the charts.

She has taken us through every stage a superstar could possibly go through and she's conquered every market along the way. She's hit the top of the charts with one of the biggest songs of all time and starred in the highest grossing film musical of all time. Olivia Newton-John's place in the record books is assured.

The 1960s

Olivia was born on September 26, 1948, in Cambridge, England. Oddly enough, Olivia wasn't born into a show business background (in fact her Welsh-born father had an academic background and her mother was the daughter of Nobel Prize winning physicist Max Borne), but somehow show business worked its way into Olivia's blood at an early age. By the time she was five, her family had moved from Wales to Australia and it was there, at Ormond College, that Olivia whittled away the hours making up songs on the piano, while her father was Master of the College.

As a child, Olivia was fascinated with the music of Slim Dusty. Slim was a rather large Australian star, who turned folk stories and lore into song. He was famous for taking his music to the people, sometimes going where there were no roads in the Australian outback. Olivia credits Dusty for her introduction into the field of country music. She also entertained friends with her own musical comedies, and by the time she was twelve years old, at her sister's insistence, she entered a local cinema contest to "find the girl who looked the most like Haley Mills." Two years later she formed a singing group with three of her friends called the Sol Four. When the group began interfering with the girls' schoolwork, it was quickly disbanded. Longing to perform, Olivia began singing in a local coffee shop owned by her sister's husband. It was a customer who suggested that Olivia should enter a contest being held by Johnny O'Keefe. She entered and won the contest, but because she was in school at the time, it would be a year before she could enjoy her prize—a trip to London.

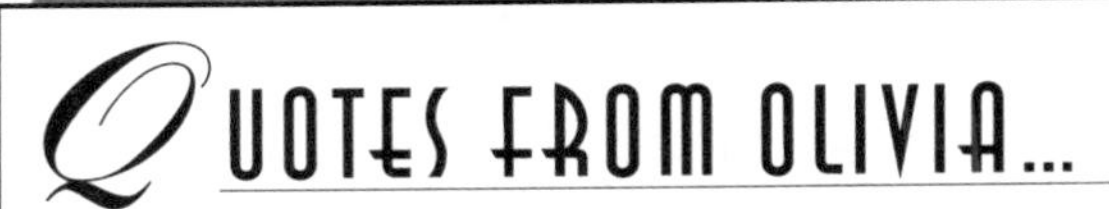

"What I wanted to do was definitely against my family tradition, and my father—who had a booming voice—let me know about it! For years, whenever I heard the classics, it always saddened me, because it was associated with disapproval."

She began her career in the late '60s in England. She seemed to crawl to stardom at a snail's pace. She formed a duo act with another Australian girl, Pat Carrol. "We sang and danced, did a lot of club work and had several spots on television," recalls Olivia. It was, in a short space of time, a successful combination. After Pat's visa ran out, she was forced to return home. Olivia's first taste of the music business was the teenybop group Toomorrow. A carefully organized creation of entrepreneur Don Kirschner (The Monkees, The Archies), it was an experience Olivia would probably like to forget. It was during this time that Olivia met Cliff Richard, England's version of Elvis. Olivia stayed to join Cliff and the Shadows on tour. Olivia credits this period as a great learning experience.

Promotional picture released by MCA Inc. in the early 1970s

THE 1970S

Promotional picture released by MCA Records

By the latter half of 1970, Olivia was a familiar fixture in the Cliff Richard group. She recorded with Cliff the first duet he ever made. The B-side, "Don't Move Away," was thought of as being superior to "Sunny Honey Girl," the A-side of the single it was released on. She remained with Cliff even after her career began rolling. Olivia signed with the Festival Records label, and released her first single "If Not For You." The song reached number seven in England, number twenty-five in the United States, and was reported as a number one smash in Italy. She also had reported success in South Africa, Belgium, and Australia. She continued touring with Cliff and appeared in his TV special "Get Away With Cliff Richard." Olivia's name became very well-known after the television show "It's Cliff Richard" hit the air. Festival Records released an album titled *If Not For You*, to follow her successful single.

From The Shadows, two men would emerge to be great influences on Olivia's career—John Rostill and John Farrar. Rostill wrote two of her biggest hits, "If You Love Me (Let Me Know)" and "Let Me Be There"; Farrar has written countless songs for Olivia throughout her career, including "Hopelessly Devoted To You" and "Magic," and eventually became her lead producer. In her dealings with The Shadows, Bruce Welch offered Olivia a role in the upcoming Cinderella pantomime. She refused the role because she wanted to return to Australia to participate in the festival season. The following year she relocated to Britain and lived with Welch (she was cited in his divorce proceedings, and the couple later got engaged). At this time, Olivia's interests away from music were "listening to records and being anywhere there is sun." She also professed to being "mad about my two red-setter dogs and horseriding."

QUOTES FROM OLIVIA...

"I don't know how much you know about me, but I'm an animal lover. Animals are so loving. and I've often thought if I could find a man who was an animal, I'd marry him in a minute."

"When I was a little girl, I really didn't have a best friend. I was always friends with the dog next door. I was always bringing home stray dogs and cats, and telling off people for mistreating animals."

"Banks Of The Ohio," Olivia's second single, went on to become a commercial success. Its ranking on the British charts landed her a Silver Disc award. Its sales were in excess of 250,000. In Australia, she received a Gold Disc award representing half a million in sales. The single also hit in Germany, South Africa, and Denmark. In 1971 and 1972, Olivia was voted the "Best British Girl Singer" by readers of the magazine *Record Mirror*. At the end of 1972, Festival Records released the album *Olivia*. Her version of George Harrison's "What Is Life" went to number ten in England. She also had a hit with "Take Me Home Country Roads," a Top 20 smash.

1972 marked a reunion of Richard, Marvin, Welch, Farrar, Newton-John and Carrol. Now Farrar's wife, Carrol rejoined her old recording partner. These partnerships took equal billing to Richard's in-concert and live albums that would follow—*Live In Japan* and *Cliff Live With Olivia Newton-John*. Olivia also participated in the 1973 Tokyo Song Festival. While Olivia was on top in Europe, her career was just beginning in the U.S. Olivia was delighted when she was asked to appear on "The Dean Martin Show" in early 1973. She was disappointed, however, that she rarely saw Mr. Martin. "He rarely comes to rehearsals," she said. "He just comes in when everything's already set up. He's so professional." Olivia received mixed reviews from the press. One comment stood out above the rest: "If white bread could sing, it would be Olivia Newton-John." Other comments such as "definitely sunny" and "wholesome" were used to describe her performances. Olivia became concerned with the comments she was receiving. She hoped her true image would eventually emerge.

While vacationing in Monte Carlo, Olivia met and fell in love with Lee Kramer, who would be her future manager. Kramer followed her back to England. Olivia left behind her engagement to Bruce Welch, and left with Kramer for the United States. She and Kramer admit it was a tempestuous, run-off relationship.

In 1973, "Let Me Be There" was released in the United States. She received rave reviews from critics and audiences alike. Olivia was amazed that the country-flavored song flew to the top of the country charts, and then to the top of the pop charts. Olivia toured the United States, and took the country by storm. She remarked that touring was so hard because of the bad food and the fact she never had a chance to sleep in her own bed. The venues were packed at her performances, and she was an easy sell at the ticket booths. While on tour, Olivia experienced one of her greatest fears. A small plane she was on had a technical difficulty and the landing gear did not come down. Fortunately, disaster was avoided—but she's had a fear of flying ever since.

Early in 1974, Olivia was chosen to participate in the Eurovision Song Festival. She was selected to represent the British market by a poll conducted on Jimmy Saville's "Club Click" on BBC-1. The poll also selected the song she would sing, "Long Live Love," and the outfit she would wear in the competition. Olivia was not pleased by either one. The British audience felt sure Olivia could easily win. The 1974 Eurovision Song Festival came and went, and she did not win. Olivia felt if she could have sung a different song and dressed more herself, she could have won.

"Do I feel that in England, I have to be the nice girl-next-door? Yes, slightly. I feel that's what people expect of me because up till now that's the image I've had. In America, my image is completely opposite to what it is here. They think of me quite differently as an artist. I'm able to be more myself. I not only have different songs, but I look different too."

Promotional picture released by MCA Records

Let Me Be There (1973)

This is the kind of music that will take you back in time and soothe your mind…Olivia Newton-John's style is modern, yet the nostalgia comes through and your memories are brought back when Olivia sings…"Help Me Make It Through The Night"…"Take Me Home Country Roads"…"Let Me Be There"…and others.

Promotional picture released by MCA Records

Promotional picture released by MCA Records

Many in England thought Olivia's remarks were very negative. While on tour in the United States, Olivia was given more of a chance to be herself and wear pants. "I wore jeans and that was exciting enough," said Olivia. "And I thought, 'they still clap and I'm wearing jeans.'" In Europe, "Take Me Home Country Roads," was released as a single. It did almost as well for her as it did for its writer, John Denver. "Have you heard her version?" Denver asked an interviewer. "The introduction comes off like gangbusters." Olivia was pleased to hear his compliment. She smiled and said, "The beginning was my idea."

1974 was a year of change for Olivia—she was fighting for acceptance on the American charts while maintaining a hold on the European charts. She won several awards in Nashville, including ones for Song of the Year and Best Female Artist. Many felt, however, that Olivia had no place in Nashville. Such greats as Dolly Parton and Johnny Paycheck rallied to stop her from receiving any further awards. Others such as Loretta Lynn said, "I've won plenty of awards over in England—so what if she wins here." Needless to say, a handful of people couldn't stop Olivia's climb to stardom.

Olivia, while touring, hosted "The Midnight Special," and appeared on "The Tonight Show with Johnny Carson." Two of her albums were released into different markets that year—*If You Love Me, Let Me Know* in the U.S.; *Long Live Love* in Europe. Both albums shared six tracks—the U.S. release contained ten tracks, while the European contained twelve, and both became commercial successes. Olivia showed the confidence that she had learned to select songs that were right for her. Her biggest successes were "If You Love Me (Let Me Know)" (which hit number five on the pop charts and number one on the country charts), "I Honestly Love You" (which hit number one on the pop and country charts), "Long Live Love" (number eleven on the pop charts) and "Changes" (a Top 40 hit).

"I've never claimed to be a country singer—to call yourself that, you have to be born into that background. I simply love country music and its straightforwardness."

"Years ago I was supposed to go to Japan on tour and I heard about a dolphin slaughter there, so I canceled a tour there. I got a lot of attention because of it. I later wrote a song about dolphins. I feel just because we're humans, we shouldn't be able to annihilate other animals, just because we're stronger."

While Olivia's country-styled songs stopped hitting in England, she gained ground on the American charts. To satisfy both markets, she began releasing albums geared towards each market. The end of 1974 marked the release of the albums titled *First Impressions* and *Music Makes My Day*. In 1975, Olivia was asked to record the only vocal track for the motion picture soundtrack "The Other Side Of The Mountain." Her single was titled "Richard's Window." The album contained two versions of the song, one of which had a vocal introduction by a star from the movie. At that time, John Denver approached Olivia to record a duet with her. She gladly accepted, especially since she had recorded several of his songs before. The single "Fly Away," climbed to the number thirteen position on the pop charts, a certified hit.

As with earlier albums, John Farrar came forward with another great song for Olivia. "Have You Never Been Mellow" was released as a single and an album, and both became commercial successes in the U.S. The title track set the mood for the rest of the album. John Denver also contributed two tracks to the project, "Good-bye Again," and "Follow Me," which were welcome additions to this collection. "Please, Mister Please" a song written by John Rostill and Bruce Welch, became one of the most memorable tracks from the album. By being placed at the end of the album, "Please" left a lasting impression on the listener.

In the late spring of 1975, Olivia took part in Paul Williams' TV special, "Listen, That's Love." Her performance was complete in itself. Paul Williams gave audiences a fuller experience than usually captured in a television special. Among the guests were Helen Reddy, Rosalind Kind, and Seals and Kroft. Though Olivia sang only one song, her presence was felt throughout the rest of the show.

The album *Clearly Love* was released internationally in 1975, and went on to be her fourth consecutive gold album. It contained such songs as "Something Better To Do" and "Let It Shine." Olivia also turned to American television to record a special, simply titled "A Special, Olivia Newton-John." Olivia took the American television audience by storm. Her guests included: Lynda Carter as her character of Wonder Woman, Lee Majors as the Six Million Dollar Man, and Rona Barrett. The success of this special led to many other appearances on television.

In Japan, a concert album and television special, both titled "Love Performance," were released. Olivia performed many of her greatest hits along with new songs. Among the songs featured were "I Honestly Love You," "Have You Never Been Mellow," "As Time Goes By," and "Please, Mister Please." Both the record and the television show were well-received.

Olivia was named 1975's Rising Star on CBS-TV's Entertainer of the Year Awards. *People* magazine ran a cover story naming Olivia the "Hottest New Pipes In Pop." That year, she also won four American Music Awards, including Favorite Pop Single–"I Honestly Love You," Top Country Album–*Let Me Be There*, Favorite Female Country Vocalist, and Favorite Female Pop Vocalist. Her awards were by no means small accomplishments, seeing that she was up against such names as Barbra Streisand, Helen Reddy, and Loretta Lynn.

As the year wore on, the Grammys came and went, leaving Olivia with the award of Best Pop Performance by a Female, along with Record of the Year for "I Honestly Love You." That same year, she was voted along with Barbra Streisand for "People's Choice for Best Loved Female Singer." Her final honor of the year came for her album *Have You Never Been Mellow*, which became her first number one album on the *Billboard* Pop Charts.

In 1976, the single "Have You Never Been Mellow" went to number one, and the album was awarded Favorite Album Pop/Rock by the American Music Awards.

Promotional picture released by MCA Records

Promotional pictures released from EMI Records Japan in 1976
to promote the Love Performance *album*

She was also honored as Favorite Female Vocalist Pop/Rock. Both the title track from *Have You Never Been Mellow*, and the single, "Please, Mister Please," achieved gold records. In the same year, Olivia recorded her first and only country album in Nashville. *Don't Stop Believin'* quieted down some of the skeptics who trashed her earlier performances because she was not American. The album spawned the international hit "Sam." A second album was released in the form of *Come On Over*. Both albums were certified gold on the United States market. She was also voted Favorite Female Vocalist Pop/Rock, and Favorite Female Vocalist by the American Music Awards.

The year 1977 marked the last year Olivia would appear on the country charts. She had new ideas in mind, the first being a brief stint into easy listening, and then onto the pop charts, and finally to disco by the end of 1978. In August of 1977, she released the album *Making A Good Thing Better*.

Olivia's breakthrough into the rock scene in 1978 was a great success that probably would not have been possible without the release of the movie *Grease*. In the movie, Olivia played Sandy, a very wholesome girl from Australia, very timid and shy and in love with a hip greaser played by John Travolta. The movie goes through their relationship and the changes Sandy makes to make him notice her. Her change from sweetheart to leather babe dictated the change in her career in the coming years. The film went on to be the most successful movie musical in history.

The soundtrack hit the number one position and stayed there for twelve weeks, and spent a total of thirty-nine weeks on the charts. The album went multi-platinum, selling eight million copies-plus. Three singles were spawned, "Hopelessly Devoted To You" (number three and gold), "You're The One That I Want" (number one, platinum, and at the time—the largest hit in the UK chart history), and "Summer Nights" (number five and gold). Allan Carr said, "Don't be fooled by that Barbie Doll adorable quality—she's a smart lady."

"We never realized the impact the film would have," said Olivia. "We went to the opening in this open-top, white '50s car. We nearly got dragged out of the car. We never knew we were putting ourselves at such risk, so after that, we used to go in a hard top."

Olivia's first rock album, *Totally Hot*, was a commercial success, and paved the way for a bright future in this new direction. It hit number seven and spent sixteen weeks on the charts. "A Little More Love" was released as her first single and went to number three and gold sales. "Deeper Than The Night," a second single, climbed to hit number eleven, and the single "Totally Hot" hit the Top 40.

Promotional picture released by MCA Records

The People's Choice Award for Favorite Motion Picture Actress of 1979 was presented to Olivia for her role of Sandy in *Grease*. Shortly afterwards, Queen Elizabeth II bestowed the OBE (Order of the British Empire) on her in a special gathering at Buckingham Palace.

Reviews — *Grease* (1978)

This adaptation of the Broadway hit is an exciting, energetic salute to the golden age of rock and roll. Exchange student Olivia Newton-John is "hopelessly devoted" to hip dragster John Travolta. Will she win his heart? Slick as a D.A., and twice as cool. *BluePrint Magazine.*

Olivia took to the studios with fellow Australian and longtime friend Andy Gibb to record two duets, "Rest Your Love On Me," and "I Can't Help It." Both appeared on Andy's album *After Dark*. They also donated their song "Rest Your Love On Me" to the UNICEF organization and performed it in a live concert of hope.

On January 9, 1979, history was made when the General Assembly Hall of the United Nations became the stage for a star-studded gathering of some of the biggest names in popular music. *The Music For Unicef Concert* featured entertainers who came together not only to celebrate the International Year Of The Child, but to launch a far-reaching fund-raising concept. Olivia performed two songs in the concert: "The Key" and "Rest Your Love On Me," the Andy Gibb duet. All royalties went to benefit the children of the world. Among the stars present were The Bee Gees, Donna Summer, Rod Stewart, and others.

Promotional picture released to promote Grease

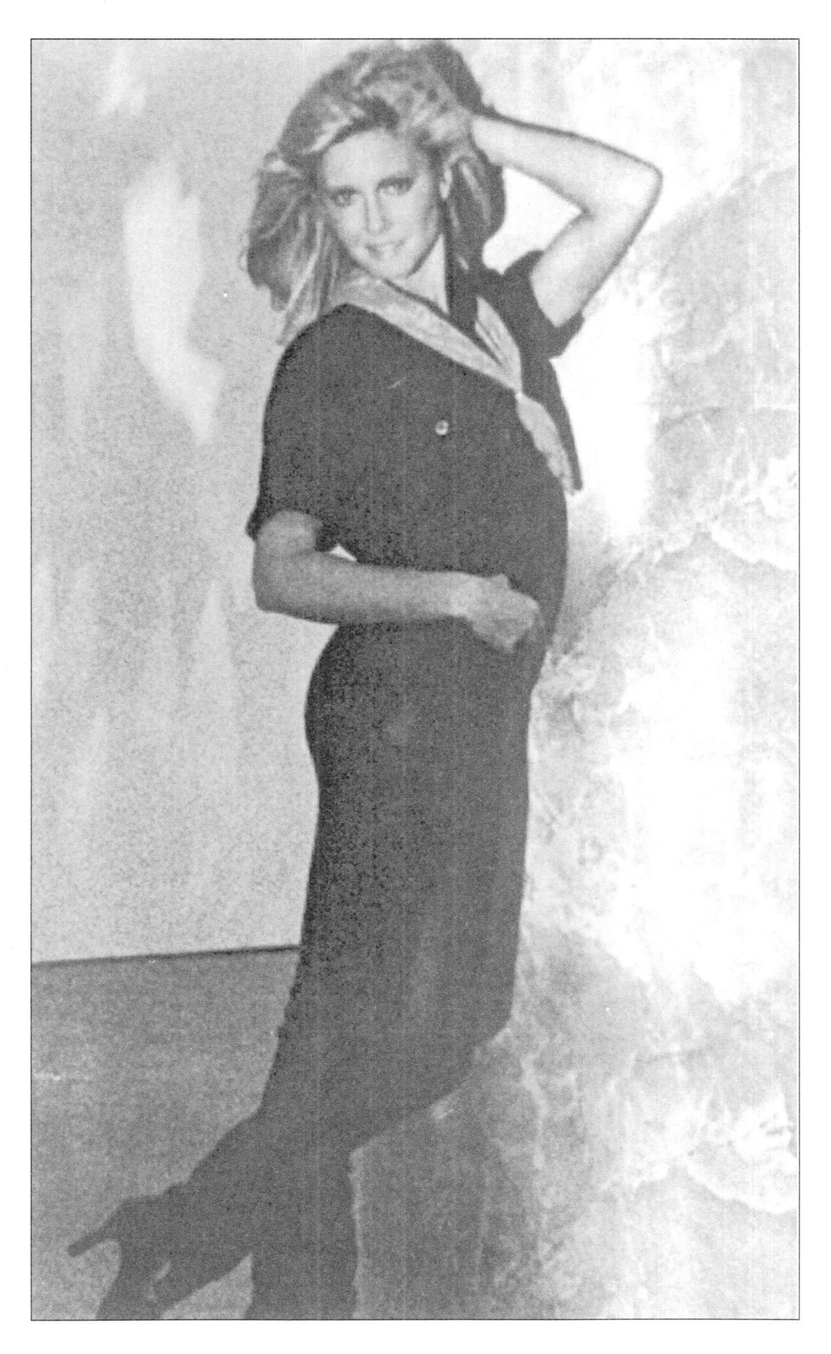

Promotional picture released by MCA Records

THE 1980S

Promotional picture released by MCA Records

UOTES FROM OLIVIA...

"If you have any preconceived ideas about me or the '80s, you better hold onto your hats."

The '80s started off on a roll for Olivia. She had her first solo starring role in the film *Xanadu*. She starred with Michael Beck and the great Gene Kelly. The story was simple—Olivia was a muse sent from Mt. Helicon to grant two dreams: for Gene Kelly, to get his big band club back, and for Michael Beck, to have success in his life. Olivia and the other eight muses were to make it happen. Of all the places to make it happen, their dreams came together in a disco roller-skating rink called *Xanadu*. The partnership in the movie was successful, the partnership in the theater was not. It fared poorly at the box office. "She's charming, lovely, and a delight to work with," said Gene Kelly of Olivia.

"My biggest flop was *Xanadu*," said Olivia. While the film flopped, the *Xanadu* soundtrack became a tremendous success. It produced for Olivia and the group ELO several Top 20 hits. The album climbed as high as number four on the charts. The singles spawned included such hits as "Magic," "Suddenly" (with Cliff Richard), "Xanadu," and "All Over The World." To promote the movie, Olivia hosted "Hollywood Nights," an all-star television special shown just before the 1980 Academy Awards, and it was packed with great entertainment. Performances of "Candle In The Wind" (Elton John and Olivia), "Suddenly" (Cliff Richard and Olivia), "I Can't Help It" (Andy Gibb and Olivia) and "Heartache Tonight" (Tina Turner, Toni Tenielle, Karen Carpenter, and Olivia), made the night outstanding.

From the ashes of *Xanadu*, Olivia went on to make up for the disastrous film. The catch phrase for 1981/1982 was "Let's Get Physical," and almost everyone did. The album spent twenty-seven weeks on the charts, peaking at number six. The single "Physical" went all the way to number one, and stayed there an amazing ten weeks. At the time, only one song by Elvis Presley was ranked higher in the record books. Other singles were released in the form of "Make A Move On Me," which rose to number five on the charts; "Landslide," which hit number fifty-two; and "Carried Away."

"Physical" inspired Olivia to take on a more sexy sultry look. The album has been referred to as "The Olivia Discovers Sex Album." This sexy image was convincingly displayed on the groundbreaking video album version of "Physical," and the television special, "Olivia Newton-John, Let's Get Physical." The video album was nominated for and won the Grammy for best long-form video. Olivia claimed another

Promotional picture from the movie Xanadu

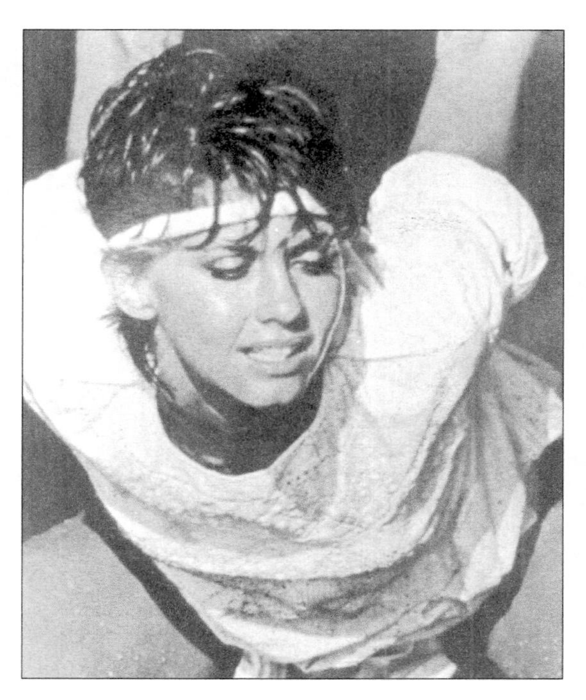

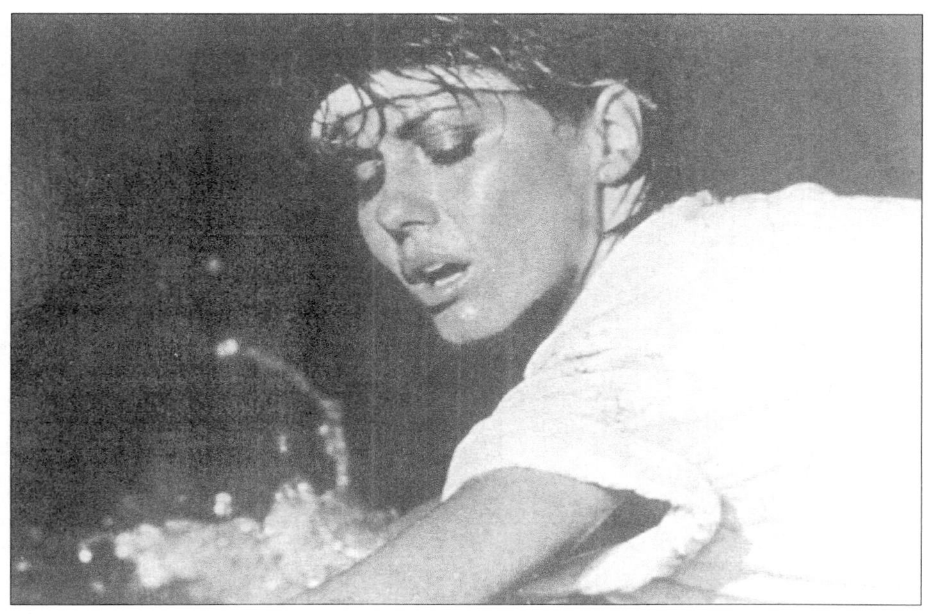

Olivia Newton-John

achievement in 1982—she was banned in Utah. The local radio stations, mostly Mormon Church members, said the song's lyrics were too suggestive and not suitable for airplay. Across the country, headlines such as "Olivia Banned," and "The Girl's A Red Hot Vamp," ran describing the banning. The small attempt to slow Olivia's success only heightened sales.

"Five years ago, I would have died over a controversy like this, but now I just think it's foolish of them to take it so seriously."

"As you get a little bit older, you get a little bit more courageous, and you stop worrying what everybody else in the world is going to think about you. You realize not everyone can like you, and there'll always be people who don't. I don't know, I think as I get older, I find the world much more interesting."

"I just wasn't in the mood for tender ballads, I wanted peppy stuff because that's how I'm feeling."

Continuing on her winning streak, and following up the success of "Physical," she released her second greatest hits collection, *Olivia's Greatest Hits Volume Two,* which quickly climbed the charts. The album contained such hits as "Hopelessly Devoted To You," "Magic," "Make A Move On Me," and "Xanadu." Two new songs were recorded for the project: "Heart Attack" and "Tied Up." The former flew up the charts to number three, the latter to the thirty-eighth position. The album went to number sixteen on the album chart and spent twenty-one weeks on the charts.

To promote *Olivia's Greatest Hits Volume Two*, she went on a tour which inspired the concert video, "Olivia In Concert." The video included such hits as: "If You Love Me (Let Me Know)," "Let Me Be There," "Physical," "Magic" and "Deeper Than The Night." Olivia's performance was wonderful and well-delivered.

While her career was running on full steam, her personal life was falling apart. She split from longtime boyfriend and manager Lee Kramer. Rumors spread about the reason why. Many believe the question of "to marry, or not to marry" was the reason. Olivia picked up and went on to enjoy her success. She made it a point in her life at this time that professional ambitions would outweigh personal relationships. No doubt when she left England and Australia, the men in her wake were a little doubtful as to the convictions of "I Honestly Love You." Many were surprised, however, that when Olivia left Lee Kramer, she decided to keep him on as a manager. Lee and Olivia had been together six years both as manager and client, and he had lived with her at her six-acre Malibu ranch.

The end of 1983 marked the release of the movie *Two Of A Kind*. The movie flopped at the box office, but the soundtrack skyrocketed and yielded more Top 40 hits for Olivia. The premise of the movie was that God was fed up with the way humans were behaving and decided to flood the Earth to get rid of them. At the last

QUOTES FROM OLIVIA...

"I'm sure both Lee and I went through every kind of emotion possible. When you live with someone for a very long time, it has to be difficult."

"We've been through a lot together, so why not? It seems a shame if after six years together, two people decide never to see each other again. It's too bad, because when a person is part of your life for so long, has watched you and shared so many things, isn't it better to be friends?"

"I thought it might be hard, but so far, it's worked out well. I hope it can continue."

"Right now I feel like I'm on a freeway, which is straight and going forward. But it has exits. And I can turn on any side road that I want. One exit I could take if I decide to, would lead to my perfect house. Lately, I've found myself doodling little pictures of cottages, with white-washed walls and picket fences. Very old fashioned, isn't that?"

"Inside the cottage I see a happy family, children. Ah, you see, you have caught me on a good day. Sometimes when the situation is bleak, I am very negative and decidedly against having children—poor things, what's the point? But this week, I've got through being depressed, and definitely want a family. But then, you have to find someone to marry first, don't you?"

"Breaking up love affairs is as low as you can get. And falling in love is as high."

minute, four angels—among them Charles Durning, Scatman Crothers, and Beatrice Straight—ask God to spare the Earth. He agrees only if they can show him two selfish people who would sacrifice themselves for each other. The people, of course, were played by Olivia and John Travolta. Their characters of Debbie and Zack, through a long chain of mishaps and trials, end up falling in love. This movie marked the first and last sex scene Olivia ever had.

From the original motion picture soundtrack, the hits "Twist Of Fate" and "(Livin' In) Desperate Times" emerged. The first just missed the top of the charts, ending up at number three. The second hit number thirty-one and the soundtrack went platinum. With the success of the platinum soundtrack came the short-form video, "Twist Of Fate." The video included the hits: "Twist Of Fate," "(Livin' In) Desperate Times," "Shaking You," "Take A Chance," "Heart Attack" and "Tied Up."

As if Olivia could do anything else to startle us, she went and did the ultimate—she got married. The man is actor Matt Lattanzi, whom she met on the set of the ill-fated *Xanadu*. Olivia defied convention by marrying a man who was ten years

Promotional picture released by MCA Records

Promotional picture released by MCA Records

JOHN TRAVOLTA OLIVIA NEWTON-JOHN
It took a Twist of Fate to make them two of a kind.
Two of a Kind

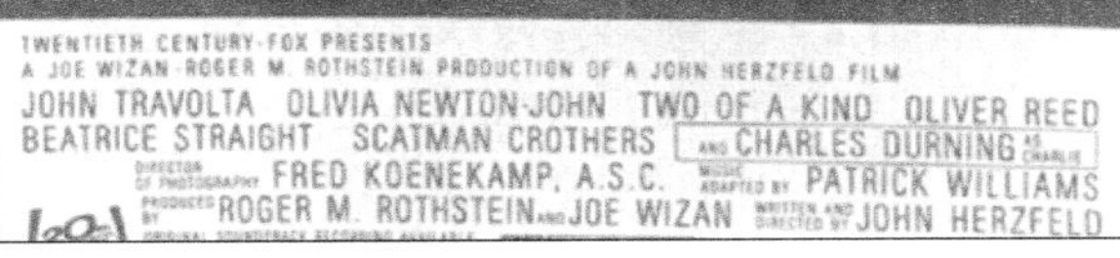
TWENTIETH CENTURY-FOX PRESENTS
A JOE WIZAN-ROGER M. ROTHSTEIN PRODUCTION OF A JOHN HERZFELD FILM
JOHN TRAVOLTA OLIVIA NEWTON-JOHN TWO OF A KIND OLIVER REED
BEATRICE STRAIGHT SCATMAN CROTHERS AND CHARLES DURNING AS CHARLIE
DIRECTOR OF PHOTOGRAPHY FRED KOENEKAMP, A.S.C.
MUSIC ADAPTED BY PATRICK WILLIAMS
PRODUCED BY ROGER M. ROTHSTEIN AND JOE WIZAN
WRITTEN AND DIRECTED BY JOHN HERZFELD

SOUL KIS
OLIVIA

Olivia Newton-John In Concert (1982)

Olivia Newton-John's concerts Friday and Saturday at Forest Hill Stadium summarized the last decade in pop, when she pulled trend after trend into the mainstream. Purists may be offended—particularly in country music, where she dallied a while—but pop singers like Miss Newton-John make new styles safe for mass audiences just as they are on the way out. At Forest Hills, she started her latest single, "Heart Attack," with punky pogo dancing, sounding a last call for the 1970s new wave.

As she might do on television, Miss Newton-John made each number a song and dance. There were costume changes, film clips, gimmicks; she sang "Silvery Rain," her anti-pesticide song in a shower of shiny confetti, and she jumped rope through "Let's Get Physical."

Miss Newton-John has a nearly colorless voice, distinguished mainly by the break between a perky chest register and a fragile head voice. Yet it is also extremely adaptable—on-stage, she summoned country's quavers, disc melismas, pop directness and hard rock's percussive staccato. She sounds delicate on her records, but she sang a 90-minute set with no obvious strain.

For all their variety, Miss Newton-John's songs have a single theme. She always plays a woman smitten with an uninterested partner and willing to make endless concessions; she sang her encore, "I Honestly Love You," on her knees. That pop persona threatens to outlast Miss Newton-John's more progressive experiments.

younger than she was. The wedding was attended mostly by family and friends. It was remarked by Olivia's father that she looked like an angel in her white gown.

In late 1985, she released the album titled *Soul Kiss*. The album started off as a success, but unfortunately it went dead in the water. Her manager at the time asked her why she got married before the album was released. The first single "Soul Kiss,"

UOTES FROM OLIVIA...

"I used to gravitate towards men who were strong, self-assured and almost arrogant. Matt is more relaxed. I was the one who had the hang-up with him being younger than me. He had no problem with it, but I did. We kept it quiet for a long time. I was kind of freaked out about it. I was afraid it wouldn't work out."

"I have a wonderful life, I realize I'm fortunate."

went to number twenty on the charts. A second, "Toughen Up," failed to chart. "I don't particularly do them because they're commercial; I think people are interested in these things," said Olivia.

A short-form video of songs from *Soul Kiss* was released. It contained five tracks from the album. As Olivia was making her last album, she was carrying a secret with her. After the release in February, she made it known she was pregnant. Twelve months after her marriage, she gave birth to her first baby girl, named Chloe Rose Lattanzi. Didn't she say to hold on to your hats?

> **Singer has baby girl**
> LOS ANGELES (AP)-It's a girl! Olivia Newton-John gave birth Friday to a five pound, six ounce girl, and the singer and her husband, actor Matt Lattanzi, named the baby Chloe, said publicist Paul Bloch. Mother and daughter were in excellent health, Bloch said. The 27-year-old Lattanzi, who starred in the 1983 film *My Tutor*, was at Miss Newton-John's side during the birth, he said. Miss Newton-John, 37, has had hits in the country and pop fields, starting with her first U.S. chartmaker, "Let Me Be There," which earned her the first of four Grammys. She also starred in the 1978 hit movie *Grease*, and met Lattanzi on the set of the movie *Xanadu* in 1980.

"As I grew older and changed, I was attracted to different music forms depending on where I was in my life and my mind, what was going on with me," said Olivia. "Now that I'm a mother, my focus is different—it's changed my direction again."

Olivia teamed up with longtime producer and friend David Foster to record the song, "The Best Of Me." The song hit the Hot 100 chart and had heavy airplay on VH-1. The song was featured on Foster's self-titled album.

Olivia was due for a comeback, and made an honest attempt to do so in 1986. The album, *The Rumour*, was released and everyone thought it would be a hit. It received rave reviews from critics, and was said to be her most mature work to date.

Olivia Down Under (1988)

Something about bicentennials brings out the dorkiest in people. I remember our 200th birthday with cringes. Now it's Australia's turn to blush. Here Olivia Newton-John pays tribute to her homeland in what HBO calls a "picture-postcard concept special."

Here's the concept: Olivia sings on tall ships, with sheep-shearers outback to muscle men on the beach and in historic Port Arthur Prison, all the time changing into lots of darling outfits. The music's fine—much of it from her new album *The Rumour*. Olivia can't be anything but cute. And the scenery is occasionally spectacular. But the bicentennial national navel-gazing does grate the senses. If only Olivia had saluted her homeland on its 201st birthday. *Grade:* B–

Promotional pictures released by MCA Records

Promotional picture released by MCA Records

Olivia wrote several of the tracks herself, and Elton John came through with the title track. As with past releases, she received poor airplay, and the first single, a dance track called "The Rumour," flopped. A second single, "Can't We Talk It Over In Bed," never made it onto the charts. The album failed to live up to expectations. The album did inspire Olivia to make another long-form video called "Olivia Down Under." It was released on HBO and then on video. Olivia was also appointed as Goodwill Ambassador to the Environment.

After seeing her last album fail on the charts, Olivia decided to do an album not aimed at the charts. Instead of rank and sales, this album was aimed at her daughter. She said she'd always wanted to do an album of lullabies since her daughter was born. When she approached MCA Records about the project, they said no. Determined to make the album, she turned her back on her record label and headed for Geffen Records. The people at Geffen thought it was a wonderful idea. She recorded the album in Australia. When the album was in production, Olivia asked if she could have the album printed on recycled paper, since she had become so environmentally conscious—and they agreed.

The first time Olivia played the album for Chloe, Olivia said that Chloe cried. It was then she knew the album was a success. She made her daughter feel important. VH-1 supported Olivia's album by filming a special called "Warm And Tender." The special contained interviews, music from the album, a trip to the rainforest to talk about the environment, and the video for "Reach Out For Me."

UOTES FROM OLIVIA...

"Before I had my baby Chloe, I used to say, and I'm embarrassed to say this now, 'What if I don't love my baby as much as I love my dog?' It sounds stupid, but when you love your animals that much you can't imagine it—but when she was born, the dog became a dog. There's nothing like it, I love it. This is the best thing in my life."

"She gets a kick out of hearing me sing, but it's nothing special to her. Sometimes she'll tease me by calling me Olivia Newton-John and then laughing."

"I wanted her to have a mother and not be raised by nannies. I had play groups at my house."

"I do have high standards, but I don't expect anything from anyone that I don't expect from myself."

"My music is a gentle way of letting people know about a situation they may not be aware of and it'll reach a wide audience. It'll reach old people, young people."

Promotional picture released by MCA Records

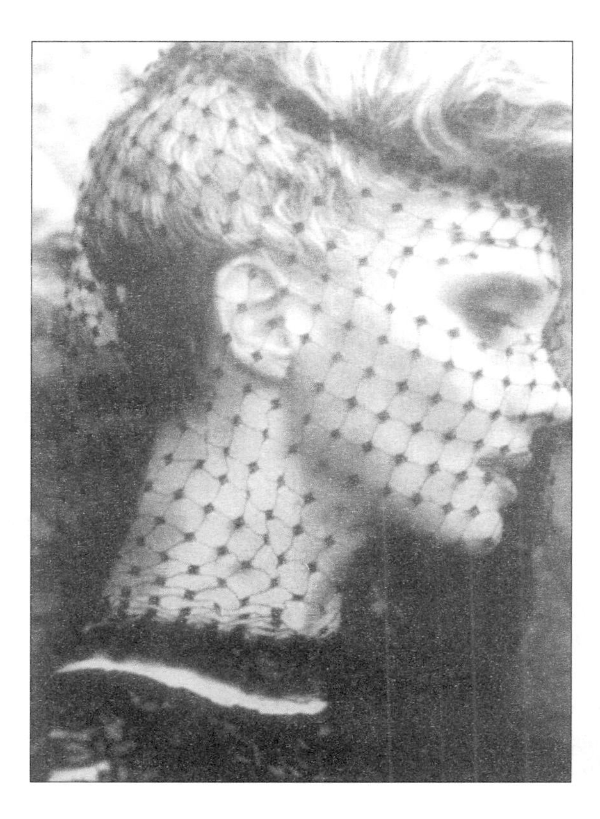

HANNA-BARBERA
PRESENTS
Timeless Tales
FROM HALLMARK
An Idea Whose
"Once Upon A Time"
Has Come!

A Golden Opportunity!
Hosted by
Olivia Newton-John

olivia · the rumour

In Japan, her continued success caused the release of the album *Early Olivia: The Past Masters*. It contained many of her early hits, as well as a few extras that deserved mention.

Timeless Tales (1988)

While Olivia Newton-John won't make anyone forget Alistair Cooke, she makes a chipper hostess for two pleasant half-hour animated tapes from Hanna-Barbera's "Timeless Tales" series. Newton-John introduces the theme: "Even a duck needs a friend, someone to tell him, 'It's okay to be different.'" Then two real children—gushing such hip words like "Radical!" and "Awesome!"—search an attic for the storybook that comes to life.

The animation is cheery, the morals aren't harped on, and Newton-John wraps up each show with a pro-environment message. The tapes are strikingly calm by comparison with most modern animated productions. So much the better. (Hanna-Barbera, $14.95 each)—*Ralph Novak*

The Rumour (1986)

It's a bit of a jolt to hear Olivia Newton-John sing about AIDS, single parenthood, and a better environment. It's as if, now that she's forty and a first-time mother herself, she suddenly cares about the world. Just as surprisingly, she connects with rock producer Davitt Sigerson's unsweetened setting and delivers believable, unstrained conviction, whether she's championing a cause, romping through the title cut (co-written by Elton John and James Newton-Howard) or exposing a vein or two on David and David's "Walk Through Fire." For eighteen years, Olivia Newton-John has been one of pop music's prettiest faces; now she just wants a little respect, and with *The Rumour* she earns it.—*Rob Hoerburger*

Ollie isn't getting physical anymore, she's getting quite mumsy, what with new child and her thriving entrepreneurial career, almost too busy to bother with the music spotlight. However, she has taken time out from changing diapers to knock this album off, and to her credit, N-J has produced quite a set of tracks. There's a new sense of maturity here. Olivia sings about domestic problems with the insight of someone who's experienced such headaches. The lyrical message of songs like "It's Not Heaven," and "Get Out" are spiced with a sense of reality only a mature person can envision. Olivia's also writing a lot more, which is another side of her expanding horizons. If there's a major fault, it is that this album has a tendency to be overproduced. Her plaintive vocal style works best when kept simple and not forced to battle against overblown arrangements. It may also have been a mistake to lead off with the Elton John-Bernie Taupin title track, definitely not the strongest cut. Yet Olivia shows enough spark here to suggest that she could handle a comeback if she made it a priority.—*Keith Sharp*

OLIVIA NEWTON-JOHN

Warm

And

Tender

Reviews — *Warm And Tender* (1989)

The combination of Newton-John's often ethereal-sounding voice and super-sweetie-pie songs could have made this album into the equivalent of a hypoglycemia attack. But she tempers the material with just enough restraint—recognizing, for instance, that nobody needs to be reminded how dreamy a tune "Over The Rainbow" is—and makes it into a long lullaby as soothing as the song suggests.

The tunes include "When You Wish Upon A Star" (sung with real attention to the lyrics), "The Twelfth Of Never" (the old Johnny Mathis hit) and Kerbfield's standard "The Way You Look Tonight," usually given a romantic interpretation but perfectly serviceable, as Newton-John proves, in a parent-child orientation.

There are also brief versions of "Rock-A-Bye-Baby," "Twinkle Twinkle Little Star," and "Brahms' Lullaby." Newton-John wrote the title song's lyrics for her daughter, who, the next time Mom gets on her case for not eating her peas, ought to quote these lines: "All my life I've waited for the angel you are/You're the dream I knew you'd be/And I love you completely my Chloe/Chloe."

So all right, the restraint breaks down from time to time. Newton-John, having bent herself out of shape once or twice trying to be a sex bomb, is certainly far more appealing when she goes all out for motherhood.—*Ralph Novak*

Promotional picture released from Geffen Records 1989

THE 1990S

Promotional picture released by MCA Records

"I really don't care if people are cynical as long as I get their attention. And even if they think I'm a jerk, I really don't particularly care."

"Pollution doesn't stop at borders; we are an endangered species. We need clean air, clean water and clean food to survive."

Olivia's Koala Blue, created in 1982 to market her line of Australian-style sportswear, went bankrupt. Owners of the franchise-style stores blamed Olivia for not supporting them. They said Olivia used her squeaky-clean image to lure investors. There were disputes between licensees and the home office because of shoddy merchandise and late deliveries—problems Olivia and Pat Farrar never solved. Olivia blamed the recession and too fast of an expansion for her chain's collapse.

Surviving the demise of her once successful business, Olivia decided to revive her film and music career. The Walt Disney Company approached her to do a made-for-TV movie. The movie, *A Mom For Christmas*, would be Olivia's first Disney project. The idea behind the movie, and from the book *A Mom By Magic*, was that a little girl makes a wish in a department store wishing well for a mom for Christmas. Her real mother had died when she was young and she lives with her workaholic father. Just before Christmas, one of the store mannequins (Olivia) comes to life to make the girl's wish come true—the problem being that mannequins don't know much and she could only stay through Christmas. As the holiday draws near, the father falls in love with the mannequin; on Christmas, though, the mannequin must return to the store—and as she begins to fade, only the love of the family can bring her back.

Olivia said she made the movie so her daughter would have some quality programming on television. The movie was a great success. Working on the set reminded Olivia of how much she wanted to work again. She announced she would soon return to the studio to work on a greatest hits collection. In Japan, Olivia's fame caused the release of another compilation, *Best Now*. This collection contained twenty of her earliest and best works.

As she was a founding member and on the board of directors of the Los Angeles-based Earth Communications Office, Olivia was a natural choice to co-host the 1990 Earth Day Special. She, along with John Denver, whom she recorded "Fly Away" with in 1975, were seen in 130 countries. The show was sponsored by UNICEF.

Olivia included herself in the AIDS awareness special "In A New Light 1992." In the program, Olivia spoke of her friend Armondo, who died of the disease. She spoke of the pain of not seeing her friend before he died, because she was pregnant, and doctors advised her against it because so little was known at the time. She spoke of the lies she told to Armondo—that she was too busy to talk to him or that she was not available. She dedicated her live performance of the song "I Honestly Love You" to his memory.

In 1992, with Olivia suffering from the demise of Koala Blue and the death of her best friend's child, Cholette Chuda, she decided to go all out to return to the music business. As plans were being set for a national concert tour, and an album of hits and four new songs was just arriving in stores, the bomb was dropped—Olivia was diagnosed with breast cancer.

Olivia's father had just died of cancer earlier that year. The album *Back To Basics: The Essential Collection 1971–1992*, sold with mediocre success. The first single spawned from the album, "I Need Love," made a small dent in the charts. A second single "Deeper Than A River," never made it into record stores. Due to the cancer shock, Olivia went into hiding, and her comeback was aborted. Olivia wanted to tell the facts about her cancer herself, before rumors got started; but even with this disclosure, stories ran rampant.

Olivia returned to the studios in 1994 to record an album of music she wrote herself. *Gaia* was released later that year. It was the first album on which she had written all the words and music herself. The first single was "No Matter What You Do."

"I'm making this information public myself, to save inquiring minds ninety-five cents."

"I am joyful—ecstatic to be alive—of course I'm not happy to have cancer."

"That day in July was the end of a lot of things for me, but I feel very happy to have discovered this cancer early. Since my operation, I have experienced nothing but an outpouring of support. George Bush sent me a sweet letter, and some of my show-biz pals sent flowers and notes. My friends and family, of course, have always been there. My husband has always supported and loved me, so it never entered my mind that he wouldn't find me attractive."

"The concern and support from total strangers has been overwhelming. I got hundreds of get-well wishes from people I never met. Some had breast cancer and wanted to share their thoughts. Others simply wanted to reach out. Their compassion means more to me than I can ever say. I draw strength from these people."

"Life is unpredictable, but you go on."

"Cancer—say the word—we've got to get used to this word. This word always freaks everybody out. It's just a word, you know. It's just a word that describes a condition. And it's not a fatal condition necessarily. I mean, strange as it may sound, it's probably the best thing that could have happened to me."

"It's called a Modified Radical, so they take a lot, but they don't take everything. So I was able to have an implant right away, which I was very fortunate. I would recommend that to many women if they have the chance. Do it, because it makes it a lot easier to go through it. They do it during surgery so they do it all at one time. You come out and you have one. You lost one and you gained a new one. It's like a new friend."

"I'm trying to be grown up about it, but I'm terrified of dying."

"I've been to hell and back, but I'm finally through the worst. I've got the cancer licked-and I'm going home. After months of going through the worst pain you could imagine, I honestly believe I'm over it."

"I'm over it as far as I'm concerned, and that's the main decision. It's the decision I've had to make."

Retreads from a singer whose pipes once promised more.

There's a hint of desperation to this album. Like her countrymen, the brothers Gibb, Newton-John never quite commuted out of the '70s and these re-release of such hits as "Sam," "Please Mister Please," "Physical," and "Magic" only raise the unfortunate question what-has-she-done-for-us-lately questions.

These were and are pleasant pop songs. On the four new tunes, Olivia sounds plaintively sweet as ever. This is certainly not an offensive album, as were her attempts to be the Queen of Kink in the mid-'80s. It's just not very interesting.—*Ralph Novak*

Promotional picture released by Geffen Records

OLIVIA AND THE ENVIRONMENT

The following is taken from an environmental pamphlet written by Olivia Newton-John:

Being a new parent brought with it new responsibilities and put my priorities in their right order. The first is to try and raise Chloe to be a good human being in a healthy environment—this is becoming more and more difficult to achieve with the garbage, air, and water pollution; deforestation; pesticides; nuclear testing; oil spills; unethical treatment of animals...and the list goes on. I was suffering from my own ecological depression and felt frustrated because I wanted to help clean up our mess but didn't know how. Then I realized there were things I could do! As a concerned mother and citizen of our beautiful planet, I put together a list of things we can practice at home that you can also do which will help to make our world green and clean for us and future generations. If we do these simple things, it will make a difference.

1

Recycle! Find a recycling center in your area or initiate one!
We have four bins: one for glass, one for paper, one for cans and one for leftovers that we put in a compost heap and use on the garden.

2

Don't use paper or plastic bags at the supermarket—take your own reusable bags or baskets. I remember how I'd laugh at my parents for saving and reusing things. We should learn and return to these habits.

3

Use as many biodegradable products as possible, such as soaps and detergents, to protect our water supply.

4

Even though it's inconvenient, use either cloth diapers or biodegradable ones—a high percentage of landfills are diapers!

5

Check labels for chlorofluorocarbons before you buy aerosol products—they destroy the ozone. Use pump action sprays instead.

6

Ask your grocer or supermarket to stock organic fruits and vegetables (grown without chemicals). If enough people ask, they'll do it! If possible, try to buy produce grown with minimal chemicals and thoroughly wash and peel everything.

7

Don't eat tuna until fishermen agree to release the dolphins that get caught in their tuna nets instead of letting them die unnecessarily. Having spent time with these wonderfully evolved creatures, I find this abhorrent. We can learn so much from them, as they are as intelligent as us, maybe more so!

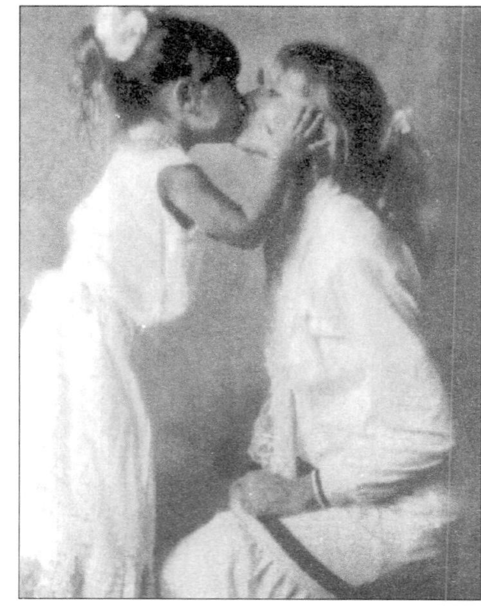

8

Don't wear real fur—it looks better on animals! Wear fake fur—it's just as warm and looks great and doesn't encourage senseless slaughtering and endangering of our animals. Also avoid using products that are inhumanely tested on animals.

9

Plant trees! We need the oxygen! I give trees as gifts and they've been some of our favorite things to receive.

10

Reduce meat consumption to help save the rainforests from being cut down for grazing cattle. Two-thirds of Central America's rainforests have been cleared to raise cattle. Eating less meat will also provide more grain to feed the starving people of the world.

Time is running out, but it's not too late! We can still save the rainforests even though, tragically, half of them have already been lost. Every hour we lose another species to extinction. Are you aware of the fact 25% of pharmaceutical drugs and cures come from rainforests? The rainforests may hold the cure for cancer or AIDS...we could lose our chance for a cure if we lose the forests.

This is just a beginning and there are many more things that you can do to help. If you would like more information send $1.00 for the "Personal Action Guide For The Earth"

To:
Friends Of The United Nations
730 Arizona Avenue
Suite 329
Santa Monica, California 90401

Let's teach ourselves and our children to value all forms of life. Let's go forward positively with love. We can and we must turn things around. We are all part of the same family—we, the trees, the plants, and the animals all live under the same sky—let's take care of our home!

From my heart to yours,
Olivia Newton-John

Promotional picture released by Geffen Records

DISCOGRAPHY

IF NOT FOR YOU (1971)

If Not For You / Me And Bobby McGee / If / Banks Of The Ohio / In A Station / Love Song / Help Me Make It Through The Night / Where Are You Going To My Love? / Lullaby / If You Could Read My Mind / If I Gotta Leave / No Regrets

Singles: If Not For You (UK #7, US #25), Banks Of The Ohio (UK #25), Love Song (did not chart)

(P) 1971 Festival Records International. D19809 Interfusion Records, England

OLIVIA (1972)

Angel Of The Morning / Just A Little Too Much / If We Only Have Love / Winterwood / My Old Man's Got A Gun / Changes / I'm A Small And Lonely Light / Why Don't You Write Me / Mary Skeffington / Behind That Locked Door / What Is Life / Everything I Own / Living In Harmony / I Will Touch You

Singles: What Is Life (UK #14), Just A Little Too Much (did not chart)

(P) 1972 Festival Records International. NSPL28168 Pye Records, England

LET ME BE THERE (1973)

Let Me Be There / Angel Of The Morning / Just A Little Too Much / Take Me Home Country Roads / Banks Of The Ohio / Me And Bobby McGee / Love Song / If Not For You / If I Could Read Your Mind / Help Me Make It Through The Night

Singles: Let Me Be There (US #6), Just A Little Too Much (did not chart), Take Me Home Country Roads (UK #15)

(P) 1973 Festival Records International. MCAD 31017 MCA Records, United States

Olivia

Olivia
Olivia Newton-John

BANKS OF THE OHIO (1973)

Angel Of The Morning / Just A Little Too Much / Take Me Home Country Roads / Banks Of The Ohio / Me And Bobby McGee / Love Song / If Not For You / If I Could Read Your Mind / Help Me Make It Through The Night

Singles: Just A Little Too Much (did not chart), Take Me Home Country Roads (UK #15)

(P) 1973 Long Island Music Company. 22533 Success, E.E.C.

CRYSTAL LADY (1974)

If Not For You / It's So Hard To Say Good-bye / Would You Follow Me / A Small And Lonely Light / Banks Of The Ohio / Where Are You Going To My Love? / Just A Little Too Much / Maybe Then I'll Think Of You / Take Me Home Country Roads / If / In A Station / Love Song / Help Me Make It Through The Night / Lullaby / If You Could Read My Mind / If I Gotta Leave / If We Only Have Love / Angel Of The Morning / My Old Man's Got A Gun / Why Don't You Write Me / Mary Skeffington / Behind That Locked Door / Living In Harmony / I Will Touch You / Heartbreaker / Rosewater / Feeling Best / Being On The Losing End / You Ain't Got The Right / Leaving / Let Me Be There / If We Try

Singles: It's So Hard To Say Good-bye (did not chart)

(P) 1974 Festival Records International. EMS 65001.2 EMI Records, Japan

LONG LIVE LOVE (1974)

Free The People / Someday / God Only Knows / Angel Eyes / Country Girl / Have Love-Will Travel / Home Ain't Home Anymore / Hands Across The Sea / The River's Too Wide / Loving You Ain't Easy / I Honestly Love You / Long Live Love

Singles: Long Live Love (UK #11), I Honestly Love You (US #1, UK #30)

(P) 1974 Festival Records International. EMC 3028 EMI Records Limited, England

OLIVIA NEWTON JOHN
BANKS OF THE OHIO
success

OLIVIA NEWTON-JOHN
LONG LIVE LOVE

CRYSTAL LADY
Olivia Newton-John
32

IF YOU LOVE ME, LET ME KNOW (1974)

If You Love Me (Let Me Know) / Free The People / God Only Knows / Mary Skeffington / Country Girl / Home Ain't Home Anymore / The River's Too Wide / I Honestly Love You / Changes / You Ain't Got The Right

Singles: If You Love Me (Let Me Know) (UK #30, US #5), I Honestly Love You (UK #30, US #1), Changes (US Top 30)

(P) 1974 Festival Records International. MCAC-411 MCA *Records, United States*

MUSIC MAKES MY DAY (1974)

Music Makes My Day / Amourese / Heartbreaker / Leaving / Feeling Best / Rosewater / Being On The Losing End / If We Try

Singles: Music Makes My Day (UK Top 30), Feeling Best (German Top 10), Rosewater (UK Top 10)

(P) Festival Records International. EMI Records International, England.

FIRST IMPRESSIONS (1974)

If Not For You / Banks Of The Ohio / Winterwood / Take Me Home Country Roads / Amourese / Let Me Be There / I Honestly Love You / Long Live Love / If You Love Me (Let Me Know) / What Is Life / If We Try / Music Makes My Day

(P) Festival Records International. D 35375 Interfusion Records, England.

if you love me
Olivia Newton-John
let me know

Olivia
Newton-John
First
Impressions

HAVE YOU NEVER BEEN MELLOW (1975)

Have You Never Been Mellow / Loving Arms / Lifestream / Goodbye Again / Water Under The Bridge / I Never Did Sing You A Love Song / It's So Easy / The Air That I Breathe / Follow Me / And In The Morning / Please, Mister Please

Singles: Have You Never Been Mellow (US #1), Please, Mister Please (US #3)

(P) 1975 EMI Records International. MCAD-1676 MCA Records Inc., United States

CLEARLY LOVE (1975)

Something Better To Do / Lovers / Slow Down Jackson / He's My Rock / Sail Into Tomorrow / Crying Laughing Loving Leaving / Clearly Love / Let It Shine / Summertime Blues / Just A Lot Of Folk (The Marshmallow Song) / He Ain't Heavy, He's My Brother

Singles: Something Better To Do (US #13), Let It Shine (US #30), He Ain't Heavy, He's My Brother (did not chart)

(P) 1975 MCA Records Inc. MCAD 31111 MCA Records, United States.

OTHER SIDE OF THE MOUNTAIN *ORIGINAL MOTION PICTURE SOUNDTRACK* (1975)

Richard's Window (two versions)

(P) 1975 MCA Records, Inc. MCAC 1539 MCA Records, United States.

Olivia Newton-John
Have You Never Been Mellow

OLIVIA NEWTON JOHN CLEARLY LOVE

'THE OTHER SIDE OF THE MOUNTAIN'
THE OTHER SIDE OF THE MOUNTAIN
COMPOSED, ARRANGED & CONDUCTED BY CHARLES FOX
MCA

COME ON OVER (1976)

Come On Over / Pony Ride / Jolene / It'll Be Me / Greensleeves / Blue Eyes Crying In The Rain / Don't Throw It All Away / Who Are You Now? / Smile For Me / Small Talk And Pride / Wrap Me In Your Arms Again / The Long And Winding Road

Singles: Come On Over (US #23), Jolene (Japan Top 10), Pony Ride (Israel Top 10)

DON'T STOP BELIEVIN' (1976)

Don't Stop Believin' / A Thousand Conversations / Compassionate Man / Newborn Babe / Hey Mr. Dreammaker / Every Face Tells A Story / Sam / Love, You Hold The Key / I'll Bet You A Kangaroo / The Last Time You Loved

Singles: Don't Stop Believin' (US #33), Sam (US #20), Every Face Tells A Story (did not chart)

MAKING A GOOD THING BETTER (1977)

Making A Good Thing Better / Slow Dancing / Ring Of Fire / Coolin' Down / Don't Cry For Me Argentina / Sad Songs / You Won't See Me Cry / So Easy To Begin / I Think I'll Say Good-bye / Don't Ask A Friend / If Love Is Real

Don't Stop Believin'

OLIVIA
NEWTON-
JOHN
MAKING
A GOOD
THING
BETTER

GREATEST HITS, VOLUME ONE (1977)

If Not For You / Changes / Let Me Be There / If You Love Me (Let Me Know) / I Honestly Love You / Have You Never Been Mellow / Please, Mister Please / Something Better To Do / Let It Shine / Come On Over / Don't Stop Believin' / Sam

(P) 1977 MCA Records, International. MCAD 5226 MCA Records, United States.

GREATEST HITS (1977)

A Window To The Sky / Feeling Best / Rosewater / If Not For You / Changes / Let Me Be There / If You Love Me (Let Me Know) / I Honestly Love You / Have You Never Been Mellow / Please, Mister Please / Something Better To Do / Let It Shine / Come On Over / Don't Stop Believin' / Sam

(P) 1977 IMD Records, Incorporated. IMD 7117 IMD Records, Japan.

GREASE
***ORIGINAL MOTION PICTURE SOUNDTRACK* (1978)**

You're The One That I Want(with John Travolta) / Hopelessly Devoted To You / We Go Together / Look At Me, I'm Sandra Dee / Summer Nights (with John Travolta)

Singles: You're The One That I Want (US #1, UK #1), Hopelessly Devoted To You (US #3), Summer Nights (US #5, UK #1), We Go Together (did not chart)

(P) 1978 RSO Records. 825 095-2 Polydor Records, United States.

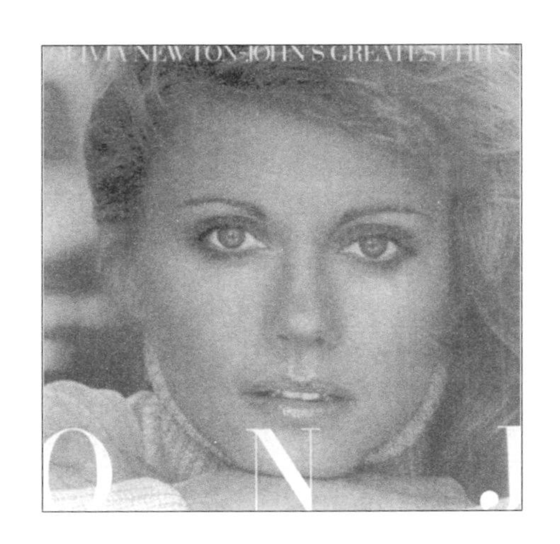
OLIVIA NEWTON-JOHN'S GREATEST HITS
O.N.J.

O.N.J.
OLIVIA NEWTON-JOHN'S
GREATEST HITS
A Window To The Sky
Pam
If You Love Me
STEREO
IMD 7117

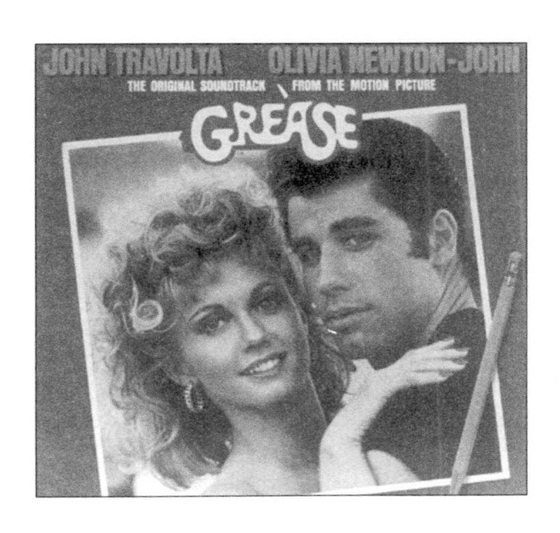
JOHN TRAVOLTA OLIVIA NEWTON-JOHN
THE ORIGINAL SOUNDTRACK FROM THE MOTION PICTURE
GREASE

TOTALLY HOT (1978)

Please Don't Keep Me Waiting / Dancin' Round And Round / Talk To Me / Deeper Than The Night / Borrowed Time / A Little More Love / Never Enough / Totally Hot / Boats Against The Current / Gimme Some Lovin'

Singles: A Little More Love (US #3), Deeper Than The Night (US #11), Totally Hot (US #32)

(P) 1978 MCA Records, Inc. MCAD 5878 MCA Records, United States.

SOUNDS LIKE OLIVIA NEWTON-JOHN (1979)

You're The One That I Want / Let Me Be There / Something Better To Do / A Little More Love / Hopelessly Devoted To You / Deeper Than The Night / Have You Never Been Mellow / Please, Mister Please / I Honestly Love You

(P) 1979 Pickwick Records. CS-3719 Pickwick Records, Canada.

THE MUSIC FOR UNICEF CONCERT: A GIFT OF SONG / THE ANDY GIBB DUETS (1979)

Rest Your Love On Me / Rest Your Love On Me (live) / The Key (live) / I Can't Help It

Singles: I Can't Help It (US #12), Rest Your Love On Me (did not chart)

(P) 1979 Polygram Distribution/ RSO Records. PD-1-6214, CT-1-3069 Polygram/ RSO, Canada/United States.

OLIVIA

Sounds Like
Olivia Newton-John
PERFORMED BY MIRROR IMAGE
HAVE YOU NEVER BEEN MELLOW
YOU'RE THE ONE THAT I WANT • LET ME BE THERE
PLEASE MR. PLEASE • HOPELESSLY DEVOTED TO YOU
SOMETHING BETTER TO DO • A LITTLE MORE LOVE
I HONESTLY LOVE YOU • DEEPER THAN THE NIGHT

ABBA
THE BEE GEES
RITA COOLIDGE
JOHN DENVER
EARTH, WIND & FIRE
THE MUSIC FOR UNICEF CONCERT
A GIFT OF SONG
ANDY GIBB
KRIS KRISTOFFERSON
OLIVIA NEWTON-JOHN
ROD STEWART
DONNA SUMMER

XANADU (1980)
Magic / Xanadu (with Electric Light Orchestra) / Suddenly (with Cliff Richard) / Dancin' (with The Tubes) / Whenever You're Away From Me (with Gene Kelly) / Suspended In Time / Fool Country / You Made Me Love You —*tracks may vary by country*

Singles: Magic (US #1), Xanadu (US #8), Suddenly (US #20)

(P) 1980 MCA Records, Inc. 465054 2 (P) 1989 CBS Records Inc, Australia.

PHYSICAL (1981)
Landslide / Stranger's Touch / Make A Move On Me / Falling / Love Make Me Strong / Physical / Silvery Rain / Carried Away / Recovery / The Promise (The Dolphin Song)

Singles: Physical (US #1), Make A Move On Me (US #5), Landslide (US #52), Carried Away (did not chart)

(P) 1981 MCA Records, International. MCAD 5229 MCA Records, Inc., United States.

PHYSICAL *EP* (1981)
Physical / The Promise (The Dolphin Song)

(P) 1981 EMI Electrola GMBH. lC 0542 EMI Records, Germany.

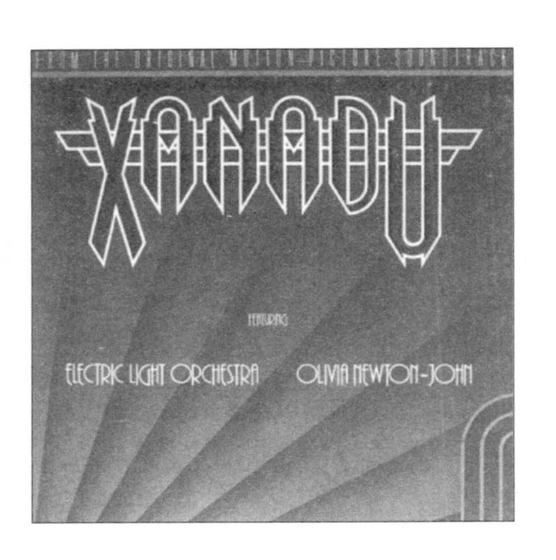
FROM THE ORIGINAL MOTION PICTURE SOUNDTRACK
XANADU
FEATURING
ELECTRIC LIGHT ORCHESTRA
OLIVIA NEWTON-JOHN

Olivia
Physical

Olivia Newton-John
PHYSICAL
12"
MAXI
SINGLE

THE BEST OF OLIVIA NEWTON-JOHN (1982)

Physical / Magic / Hopelessly Devoted To You / Make A Move On Me / A Little More Love / Carried Away / Rest Your Love On Me (with Andy Gibb) / Let It Shine / Let Me Be There / If Not For You / If You Love Me (Let Me Know) / I Honestly Love You / Have You Never Been Mellow / Please, Mister Please / Don't Stop Believin' / Sam / You're The One That I Want / Suddenly / Xanadu

(P) 1982 Music Star. MS 8197 Music Star, Maylasia.

GREATEST HITS VOLUME TWO (1982)

Heart Attack / Magic / Physical / Hopelessly Devoted To You / Make A Move On Me / A Little More Love / Tied Up / You're The One That I Want / Suddenly / Xanadu

Singles: Heart Attack (US #3), Tied Up (US #38)

(P) 1982 MCA Records, Inc. MCAD 5347 MCA Records, United States.

GREATEST HITS, *ENGLAND* (1982)

What Is Life / Take Me Home Country Roads / Changes / I Honestly Love You / Heart Attack / Magic / Physical / Hopelessly Devoted To You / Make A Move On Me / A Little More Love / Tied Up / You're The One That I Want / Suddenly / Xanadu

Singles: Heart Attack (UK Top 10)

(P) 1982 EMI Records. GO 8210 GL EMI Records Ltd., England

IF NOT FOR YOU
PHYSICAL
XANADU
MAGIC
SAM
THE BEST OF

Olivia's Greatest Hits Vol 2

Olivia's
Greatest
Hits

OLIVIA'S GREATEST HITS, VOLUME THREE (1982)
Totally Hot / Deeper Then The Night / The Promise / Landslide / Heart Attack / Magic / Physical / Hopelessly Devoted To You / Make A Move On Me / A Little More Love / Tied Up / You're The One That I Want / Suddenly / Xanadu

(P) 1982 ONJ Productions Inc. D52015 Interfusion Records, England.

OLIVIA IN CONCERT (1982)
Deeper Then The Night / Heart Attack / Magic / Physical / Hopelessly Devoted To You / Make A Move On Me / A Little More Love / Jolene / Silvery Rain / Falling / If You Love Me / I Honestly Love You / Please, Mister Please / Sam / You're The One That I Want / Suddenly / Xanadu

(P) 1982 MCA Video, Inc. 55124 MCA Records, United States.

OLIVIA'S GREATEST HITS, *ISRAEL* (1982)
Pony Ride / Boats Against The Current / Come On Over / Totally Hot / Heart Attack / Magic / Physical / Hopelessly Devoted To You / Make A Move On Me / A Little More Love / Tied Up / You're The One That I Want / Suddenly / Xanadu

(P) 1982 747 Pop. 8200 747 Records, Israel.

Olivia's Greatest Hits Vol. 3

OLIVIA
STEREO
IN CONCERT

OLIVIA'S NEWTON-JOHN
Olivia's Greatest Hits
8200

ANGEL OF THE MORNING (1982)

Let Me Be There / Angel Of The Morning / Just A Little Too Much / Take Me Home Country Roads / Banks Of The Ohio / Me And Bobby McGee / Love Song / If Not For You / If I Could Read Your Mind / Help Me Make It Through The Night

(P) 1982 OJN Records. TLA-50137 TLA Records, United States.

THE BEST OF (1982)

Let Me Be There / Angel Of The Morning / Just A Little Too Much / Take Me Home Country Roads / Banks Of The Ohio / Me And Bobby McGee / Love Song / If Not For You / If I Could Read Your Mind / Help Me Make It Through The Night

(P) 1982 TLA Records. AG 3308 TLA Records, United States.

SUPERSTARS (with Tom Jones) (1982)

Angel Of The Morning / Just A Little Too Much / Banks Of The Ohio / Me And Bobby McGee / If I Could Read Your Mind / Help Me Make It Through The Night

(P) 1982 Entrophy Record Co. TLA 50138 TLA Records, United States.

OLIVIA NEWTON-JOHN
Angel Of the Morning

The Best of
OLIVIA NEWTON-JOHN
T.L.A.

Olivia NEWTON-JOHN
& Tom JONES
SUPER STARS

TOM AND OLIVIA (with Tom Jones) (1982)
Take Me Home Country Roads / Banks Of The Ohio / Love Song / If Not For You

(P) 1982 351 Record Company, Inc. TLA-50139 TLA Records, United States.

TWO OF A KIND / TWIST OF FATE *EP* (1983)
Twist Of Fate / (Livin' In) Desperate Times / Take A Chance (with John Travolta) / Shaking You / Heart Attack / Tied Up —*tracks vary per title*

Singles: Twist Of Fate (US #3), (Livin' In) Desperate Times (US #31)

(P) 1983 MCA Records, Inc. MCAC 6127 MCA Records, United States.

TWIST OF FATE *12"* (1983)
Twist Of Fate (remix) / Twist Of Fate (album version)

(P) 1983 MCA Records, Inc. MCA 3729 MCA Records, United States.

Tom Jones & Olivia Newton-John
TOM
& OLIVIA

JOHN TRAVOLTA OLIVIA NEWTON-JOHN
TWO OF A KIND

OLIVIA
TWIST OF FATE

(LIVIN' IN) DESPERATE TIMES *12"* (1984)
Twist Of Fate (remix) / (Livin' In) Desperate Times (remix long version)

(P) 1984 MCA Records, Inc. MCA 3775 MCA Records, United States.

SOUL KISS (1985)
Soul Kiss / Toughen Up / Queen Of The Publication / Emotional Tangle / Culture Shock / Moth To A Flame / Love You Were Great, How Was I? (with Carl Wilson) / Driving Music / The Right Moment / Electric

Singles: Soul Kiss (US #20), Toughen Up (did not chart)

(P) 1985 MCA Records, Inc. MCAD 6151 MCA Records, United States.

SOUL KISS *12"* (1985)
Soul Kiss (dub mix) / Soul Kiss (remixed version) / Soul Kiss (instrumental) / Soul Kiss (short edit) / Electric —*tracks may vary per country*

(P) 1985 Olivia Newton-John. MERX 210 (884 090-1) Mercury Records, England

OLIVIA
LIVIN' IN DESPERATE TIMES

OLIVIA

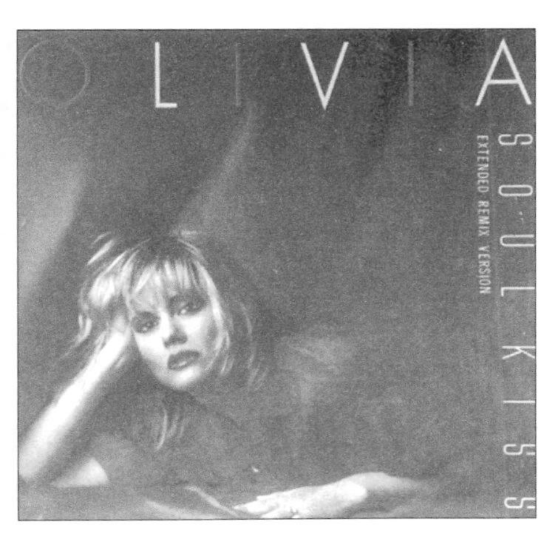
OLIVIA
SOUL KISS
EXTENDED REMIX VERSION

TOUGHEN UP *12"* (1985)

Toughen up (dub mix) / Toughen Up (remix version) / Toughen Up (single version), Car Games *—tracks may vary per country*

(P) 1985 MCA Records, Inc. 23606 MCA Records, United States.

THE RUMOUR *EP* (1988)

The Rumour (extended mix) / The Rumour (album mix) / The Rumour (remixed edit) / Winter Angel *—tracks may vary per country*

(P) 1988 MCA Records, Inc. CD45-17594 Promotional, MCA Records, United States.

THE RUMOUR (1988)

The Rumour / Love And Let Live / Can't We Talk It Over In Bed? / Let's Talk About Tomorrow / It's Not Heaven / Walk Through Fire / Big And Strong / Get Out / Car Games / Tutta La Vita / Winter Angel, It's Always Australia For Me
—tracks may vary per country

Singles: The Rumour (US #62), Can't We Talk It Over In Bed? (did not chart)

(P) 1988 MCA Records, Inc. MCAD 6245 MCA Records, United States.

OLIVIA
TOUGHEN UP

Olivia · the rumour

Olivia · the rumour

OLIVIA DOWN UNDER VIDEO (1989)

Click Go The Shears / Old Fashioned Man / It's Always Australia To Me / The Rumour / Love And Let Live / Can't We Talk It Over In Bed / Let's Talk About Tomorrow / It's Not Heaven / Walk Through Fire / Big And Strong / Get Out / Car Games / Tutta La Vita / Winter Angel

(P) 1989 Polygram Video, Inc. 080 601-3 Polygram Video.

WARM AND TENDER (1989)

Jenny Rebecca / Rocking / The Way You Look Tonight / Lullaby, Lullaby My Lovely One / You'll Never Walk Alone / Sleep My Princess / The Flower That Shattered The Stone / Twinkle, Twinkle Little Star / Warm And Tender / Rock A Bye Baby / Over The Rainbow / The Twelfth Of Never / All The Pretty Little Horses / When You Wish Upon A Star / Reach Out For Me (w/ Brahms' Lullaby)

(P) 1989 Geffen Records. 9 24257-2 Geffen, United States.

SELECTIONS FROM WARM AND TENDER (1989)

Reach Out For Me (short form) / The Twelfth Of Never

(P) 1989 Geffen Records. PRO-C 3857 Geffen, United States.

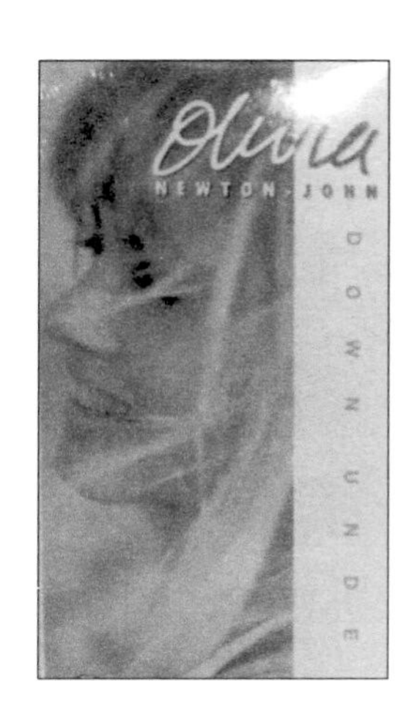
Olivia
NEWTON-JOHN
DOWN UNDE

OLIVIA NEWTON-JOHN

OLIVIA NEWTON-JOHN
Selections From
WARM AND TENDER

SPIRIT OF THE FOREST *EP* (1989)

Spirit Of The Forest (12" Mix) / Spirit Of The Forest (12" AA) / Spirit Of The Forest (12" A)

(P) 1989 Virgin Records. 7 96551-0 Virgin Records, United States.

EARLY OLIVIA: THE PAST MASTERS (1990)

If Not For You / Banks Of The Ohio / Take Me Home Country Roads / Help Me Make It Through The Night / Let Me Be There / Love Song / What Is Life / The Air That I Breathe / Me And Bobby McGee / Music Makes My Day / Long Live Love / If You Love Me / Have You Never Been Mellow / Please, Mister Please / I Honestly Love You

(P) 1990 EMI Records International. CP21-6072 EMI Records, Japan.

BEST NOW (1991)

If Not For You / Banks Of The Ohio / Take Me Home Country Roads / Help Me Make It Through The Night / Let Me Be There / Love Song / What Is Life / Me And Bobby McGee / Long Live Love / If You Love Me / Have You Never Been Mellow / Please Mister Please / I Honestly Love You / Changes / Angel Of The Morning / Follow Me / It's So Easy / If / If You Could Read My Mind / Everything I Own

(P) 1991 EMI Records International. TOCP-9084 EMI Records, Japan.

Spirit of the Forest: Africa Bambaataa, Jon Anderson, B.52's, Michael de Barre, Big Country – Mark Brezezicki, Lisa Bonet, Brother Beyond – Nathan Moore, Sam Brown, Kate Bush, Belinda Carlisle, David Clayton Thomas, Rita Coolidge, Lacy J. Dalton, Taylor Dayne, Thomas Dolby, Escape Club – Trevor Steele, Andy Fairweather Lowe, Fish, Fleetwood Mac – Mick Fleetwood, Billy Burnette, Bruce Foxton, Gentlemen Without Weapons, Louise Goffin, Debbie Harry, Richie Havens, It Bites – Frank Dunnery, Marc Jordan, The Jungle Brothers, Lenny Kravitz, LL Cool J, Little Steven, Dolette McDonald, Mr. Mister – Richard Page, Joni Mitchell, Olivia Newton-John, Pink Floyd – David Gilmour, The Plasmatics, Iggy Pop, Raging Hormones, Bonnie Raitt, The Ramones, Chris Rea, Shikisha, Amy Sky, Ringo Starr, Donna Summer, Johnny Warman, Was Not Was, Kim Wilde, Brian Wilson, XTC.

OLIVIA NEWTON-JOHN
Early Olivia

BEST NOW
OLIVIA NEWTON-JOHN

TWIN BEST NOW (1992)

If Not For You / A Small And Lonely Light / Banks Of The Ohio / Where Are You Going To My Love? / Just A Little Too Much / Take Me Home Country Roads / If / Love Song / Help Me Make It Through The Night / Lullaby / If You Could Read My Mind / If I Gotta Leave / If We Only Have Love / Angel Of The Morning / My Old Man's Got A Gun / Why Don't You Write Me / Mary Skeffington / Behind That Locked Door / Living In Harmony / I Will Touch You / Rosewater / Let Me Be There / Music Makes My Day / In A Station / No Regrets / Winterwood / Loving Arms / Lifestream / Good-bye Again / Water Under The Bridge / I Never Did Sing You A Love Song / It's So Easy / Follow Me / Changes / The Air That I Breathe / And In The Morning / What Is Life / Everything I Own / Me And Bobby McGee / Long Live Love / Have You Never Been Mellow / Please, Mister Please / I Honestly Love You

(P) 1992 EMI Records International. TOCP-7321-22 EMI Records, Japan.

BACK TO BASICS: THE ESSENTIAL COLLECTION 1971-1992 (1992)

I Need Love / Deeper Than A River / I Want To Be Wanted / Not Gonna Be The One / Twist Of Fate / Summer Nights / Have You Never Been Mellow / Deeper Then The Night / Magic / Physical / Hopelessly Devoted To You / A Little More Love / If You Love Me / I Honestly Love You / Please Mister Please / Sam / You're The One That I Want

Singles: I Need Love (US Hot 100), Deeper Than A River (did not chart)

(P) 1992 Geffen Records. GEFD-24470 Geffen Records, United States.

I NEED LOVE *EP* (1992)

I Need Love (dance mix) / I Need Love (extended mix) / I Need Love (album mix) / I Need Love (A Deeper Need Of Love mix) / I Need Love (instrumental) / The Rumour (Shep Pettibone mix) / Physical / Sam / Warm And Tender —*tracks may vary per country*

(P) 1992 Geffen Records. GEFDM-21814 Geffen Records, United States.

TWIN
BEST NOW
OLIVIA NEWTON JOHN

Olivia
Newton
John

OLIVIA
I NEED LOVE

THE GREATEST HITS COLLECTION (1994)
I Need Love / Deeper Than A River / Not Gonna Be The One / The Rumour / Soul Kiss / Suddenly / Summer Nights / Xanadu / Have You Never Been Mellow / Magic / Physical / Hopelessly Devoted To You / If Not For You / Take Me Home Country Roads / What Is Life / Banks Of The Ohio / A Little More Love / I Honestly Love You / Sam / You're The One That I Want

(P) 1994 Geffen Records. GEFD-24470 Geffen, United States.

THE EMI COUNTRY MASTERS SERIES: 48 ORIGINAL TRACKS (1994)
Music Makes My Day / No Regrets / Winterwood / The Air That I Breathe / What Is Life / Everything I Own / Have You Never Been Mellow / Please Mister Please / I Honestly Love You / If You Love Me / Hands Across The Sea / Have Love-Will Travel / Loving You Ain't Easy / You Ain't Got The Right / Country Girl / Rosewater / Country Girl / Heartbreaker / Amourese / If Not For You / It's So Hard To Say Good-bye / Would You Follow Me / A Small And Lonely Light / Banks Of The Ohio / Where Are You Going To My Love? / Just A Little Too Much / Maybe Then I'll Think Of You / Take Me Home Country Roads / If / In A Station / Love Song / Help Me Make It Through The Night / Lullaby / If You Could Read My Mind / If I Gotta Leave / If We Only Have Love / Angel Of The Morning / My Old Man's Got A Gun / Why Don't You Write Me / Mary Skeffington / Behind That Locked Door / Living In Harmony / I Will Touch You / Heartbreaker / Rosewater / Feeling Best / Being On The Losing End / You Ain't Got The Right / Leaving / Let Me Be There

(P) 1994 EMI Records International. 7243 8 27110 2 5 EMI Records, United States.

THE GRAMMYS GREATEST MOMENTS, VOLUME 3 (1994)
A live performance of "Hopelessly Devoted To You" from 21st Annual Grammy Awards, February 15, 1979.

(P) 1994 Atlantic Records. 82576-2 Atlantic, United States.

THE GREATEST HITS COLLECTION 1971 - 1994
Olivia
Newton-John

OLIVIA NEWTON-JOHN
48 ORIGINAL
TRACKS

GRAMMY'S
GREATEST
MOMENTS

GAIA: ONE WOMAN'S JOURNEY (1994)

Trust Yourself / No Matter What You Do / No Other Love / Pegasus / Why Me / I Never Knew Love / Silent Ruin / Not Gonna Give Into It / The Way Of Love / Don't Cut Me Down / Gaia / Do You Feel

Singles: No Matter What You Do

(P) 1994 ONJ Productions, USA. TVD 93406 (RMD 53406) Festival Records PTY Limited, Australia

CONDENSED ALBUM LISTING

The International Album Collection

If Not For You
Olivia
Olivia Newton-John
Cliff Live With Olivia Newton-John
Let Me Be There
Banks Of The Ohio
Music Makes My Day
First Impressions
If You Love Me, Let Me Know
Long Live Love
Crystal Lady
Have You Never Been Mellow
Clearly Love
Come On Over
Don't Stop Believin'
Making A Good Thing Better
Totally Hot
Physical
Physical *EP*
Tom And Olivia (*with Tom Jones*)
Superstars (*with Tom Jones*)
Angel Of The Morning
Two Pack Collections:
- If You Love Me, Let Me Know / Let Me Be There
- Have You Never Been Mellow / Don't Stop Believin'
- Come On Over / Clearly Love
- First Impressions / Making A Good Thing Better
- Don't Stop Believin' / Totally Hot

Twist Of Fate *EP*
(Livin' In) Desperate Times *EP*
Soul Kiss
Soul Kiss *EP*
Toughen Up *EP*
Spirit Of The Forest *EP*
Warm And Tender
Selections From Warm And Tender
Reach Out For Me *EP*
When You Wish Upon A Star *EP*
Gaia
Japanese Box Set (*10 LPs and promotional materials*)

The Greatest Hits Collection

Greatest Hits Volume One
Stars And Schlager *Germany*
Greatest Hits *Japan*
Sounds Like Olivia Newton-John
The History Of Olivia Newton-John
The Best Of Olivia Newton-John *American*
The Best Of Olivia Newton-John *Maylasia*
Greatest Hits *England*
Greatest Hits Two *Japan*
Greatest Hits Volume Two
Greatest Hits Volume Three
Olivia Greatest Hits *Israel*
Early Olivia: The Past Masters
Superstar Hit Collection *Japan*
Best Now *Japan*
Twin Best Now *Japan*
Super Best *Japan*
Back To Basics: The Essential Collection 1971-1992
Love Songs
Greatest Hits *Indonesia*
EMI Country Masters: 48 Original Tracks
The Greatest Hits Collection 1971-1994
Greatest Hits-First Impressions
Greatest Hits Volume Two Australia

Soundtracks

Toomorrow (1970)
Other Side Of The Mountain (1975)
Grease (1978)
Xanadu (1980)
Two Of A Kind (1983)
Down Under (1988)
A Mom For Christmas (1990)
Grease Mega-Mix (1994)

CONCERT LISTING

Concerts

LOVE PERFORMANCE *JAPAN* (1976)

Jolene / Take Me Home Country Roads / Don't Stop Believin' / Let Me Be There / Pony Ride / As Time Goes By / Never The Less / My Love Is Alive / Newborn Babe / Have You Never Been Mellow / If You Love Me (Let Me Know) / I Honestly Love You / The Air That I Breathe / Something Better To Do

A GIFT OF SONG THE MUSIC FOR UNICEF CONCERT (1978)

The Key / Rest Your Love On Me

OLIVIA IN CONCERT (1983)

Deeper Then The Night / Heart Attack / Magic / Physical / Hopelessly Devoted To You / Make A Move On Me / A Little More Love / Jolene / Silvery Rain / Falling / If You Love Me / I Honestly Love You / Please, Mister Please / Sam / You're The One That I Want / Suddenly / Xanadu

RADIO SHOWS LISTING

Radio Shows

COUNTRY COOKIN' (1975)
One-sided record show

MAKING A GOOD THING BETTER (1980)
NBC RADIO SHOW
Two records

SPOTLIGHT SPECIAL (1983)
Two records

STAR TRAK PROFILE (1987)
Four records

Picture Disc Listing

Picture Discs

THE RUMOUR
LP
Germany (1988)

XANADU
LP
United States (1980)
(rarest Olivia in existence—only 39 made)

MAGIC
7" Single
United States (1980)

DEEPER THAN THE NIGHT
7" Single
United States (1978)

TOTALLY HOT
LP
United States (1978)

Xanadu - Rarest Olivia Record In The World!! Ultra Rare 10" Picture Disc Prototype From Xanadu Soundtrack. Only 39 In Existence! Never Released As A Promo Because The Project Was Cancelled!

Promotional picture released by MCA Records

SINGLES LISTING

The International Singles Collection

ROLL LIKE A RIVER/
I COULD NEVER
(with the Group Toomorrow)

TILL YOU SAY YOU'LL BE MINE
(with the Group Toomorrow)

DON'T MOVE AWAY/
SUNNY HONEY GIRL
(with Cliff Richard)
EMI Records

IF NOT FOR YOU/
THE BIGGEST CLOWN
UNI Records 1971 55281

BANKS OF THE OHIO/
LOVE SONG
UNI Records 1971

IT'S SO HARD TO SAY GOOD-BYE/
BANKS OF THE OHIO
UNI Records 1971 55304

WHAT IS LIFE/
I'M A SMALL AND LONELY LIGHT
UNI Records 1972 55317

JUST A LITTLE TOO MUCH/
MY OLD MAN'S GOT A GUN
UNI Records 1973 55348

TAKE ME HOME COUNTRY ROADS/
SAME
Festival Records 1973

LET ME BE THERE/
MAYBE THEN I'LL THINK OF YOU
MCA Records 1973 MCA-40101

IF YOU LOVE ME (LET ME KNOW)/
BROTHERLY LOVE
MCA Records 1974 MCA-40209

MUSIC MAKES MY DAY/
SAME
EMI Records 1974

LONG LIVE LOVE/
ANGEL EYES
EMI Records 1974

I HONESTLY LOVE YOU/
HOME AIN'T HOME ANYMORE
MCA Records 1974 MCA 40208

CHANGES/
SAME
MCA Records 1974

ROSEWATER/
SAME
EMI Records 1974

WINTERWOOD/
SAME
EMI Records 1974

HAVE YOU NEVER BEEN MELLOW/
WATER UNDER THE BRIDGE
MCA Records 1975 MCA-40349

PLEASE, MISTER PLEASE/
AND IN THE MORNING
MCA Records 1975 MCA-40418

FLY AWAY
(with John Denver)
RCA Records 1975

LET IT SHINE/
HE AIN'T HEAVY, HE'S MY BROTHER
MCA Records 1975 MCAD-40495

SOMETHING BETTER TO DO/
HE'S MY ROCK
MCA Records 1975 MCAD-40459

JOLENE/
WRAP ME IN YOUR ARMS AGAIN
EMI Records 1976 Japan

HE AIN'T HEAVY, HE'S MY BROTHER/
SAME
EMI Records 1976

COME ON OVER/
SMALL TALK AND PRIDE
MCA Records 1976 MCA-40525

EVERY FACE TELLS A STORY/
LOVE, YOU HOLD THE KEY
MCA Records 1976 MCA-40642

DON'T STOP BELIEVIN'/
GREENSLEEVES
MCA Records 1976 MCA-40600

SAM/
I'LL BET YOU A KANGAROO
MCA Records 1976 MCA-40670

MAKING A GOOD THING BETTER/
SAME
MCA Records 1977

YOU'RE THE ONE THAT I WANT/
ALONE AT THE DRIVE IN
(with John Travolta)
RSO Records 1978 RS 891

I HONESTLY LOVE YOU/
DON'T CRY FOR ME ARGENTINA
MCA Records 1978 MCA-40811

SUMMER NIGHTS/
ROCK AND ROLL PARTY QUEEN
(with John Travolta)
RSO Records 1978 RS 906

HOPELESSLY DEVOTED TO YOU/
LOVE IS A MANY SPLENDORED THING
RSO Records 1978 RS 903

A LITTLE MORE LOVE/
BORROWED TIME
MCA Records 1978 MCA-40975

DEEPER THAN THE NIGHT/
PLEASE DON'T KEEP ME WAITING
MCA Records 1978 MCA-41009

TOTALLY HOT/
DANCIN' ROUND AND ROUND
MCA Records 1979 MCA-41074

I CAN'T HELP IT/
SOMEONE I AIN'T
(with Andy Gibb)
RSO Records 1979 RS 1026

REST YOUR LOVE ON ME/
SAME
(with Andy Gibb)
RSO Records 1979 Maylasia

MAGIC/
FOOL COUNTRY
MCA Records 1980 MCA-41247

XANADU/
WHENEVER YOU'RE AWAY FROM ME
(with ELO / Gene Kelly)
MCA Records 1980 MCA-41285

SUDDENLY/
YOU MADE ME LOVE YOU
(with Cliff Richard)
MCA Records 1980 MCA-51007

PHYSICAL/
THE PROMISE
MCA Records 1981 MCA-51182

MAKE A MOVE ON ME/
FALLING
MCA Records 1981 MCA 52000

LANDSLIDE/
RECOVERY
MCA Records 1982 MCA-51155

CARRIED AWAY/
SAME
Music Star Records 1982 Maylasia

HEART ATTACK/
STRANGER'S TOUCH
MCA Records 1982 MCA-52100

TIED UP/
SILVERY RAIN
MCA Records 1982 MCA-52155

TWIST OF FATE/
TAKE A CHANCE
(with John Travolta)
MCA Records 1983 MCA-52284

(LIVIN' IN) DESPERATE TIMES/
LANDSLIDE
MCA Records 1984 MCA-52341

SOUL KISS/
ELECTRIC
MCA Records 1985 MCA-52686

TOUGHEN UP/
DRIVING MUSIC
MCA Records 1986 MCA-52757

THE BEST OF ME/
SAJE'
(with David Foster)
Atlantic Records 1986 7-89420

THE RUMOUR/
THE RUMOUR (REMIX)/
WINTER ANGEL
MCA Records 1988 MCA-53294

CAN'T WE TALK IT OVER IN BED/
GET OUT
Interfusion Records 1988 MX-70331

THE SPIRIT OF THE FOREST/
SAME
Virgin Records 1989

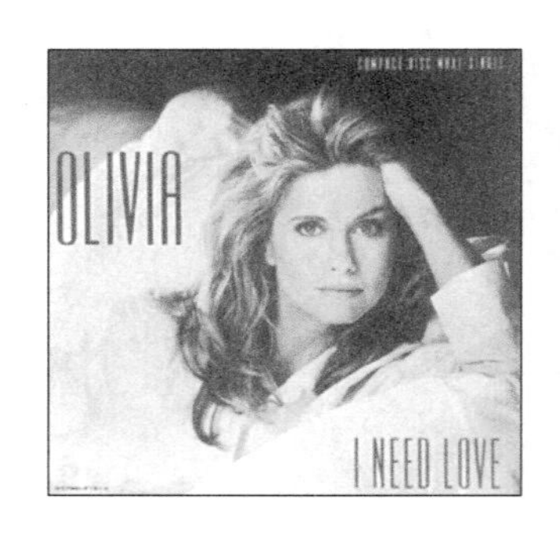

REACH OUT FOR ME/
THE FLOWER THAT SHATTERED THE STONE
Geffen Records 1989

WHEN YOU WISH UPON A STAR/
SAME
EMI Records 1990

I NEED LOVE/
I NEED LOVE (*REMIX*)/
WARM AND TENDER
Geffen 1992

DEEPER THAN A RIVER/
DEEPER (*REMIX*)
Geffen 1992

FACE TO FACE/
SAME
(with Barry Gibb)
1992

NO MATTER WHAT YOU DO/
SILENT RUIN
Festival Records 1994
D11769 ON.J Productions

TV AND VIDEO LISTING

The International Television and Video Collection

THE BEST OF THE MIDNIGHT SPECIAL (1974)
Olivia hosted and performed live tracks, including: "If You Love Me (Let Me Know)," "You Ain't Got The Right," and "I Honestly Love You."

THE BEST OF THE MIDNIGHT SPECIAL (1975)
Olivia performed live versions of the songs from her album *Have You Never Been Mellow*. Songs included: "Have You Never Been Mellow," "The Air That I Breathe," and "I Never Did Sing You A Love Song."

THE BEST OF THE MIDNIGHT SPECIAL (1975)
Olivia performed tracks from the album *Clearly Love*. Songs included: "Let It Shine," "The Long And Winding Road," and "Have You Never Been Mellow."

THE BEST OF THE MIDNIGHT SPECIAL (1976)
Olivia hosted and performed music from her album *Don't Stop Believin'*.

A SPECIAL, OLIVIA NEWTON-JOHN (1976)
Olivia took to American television for her first special, simply titled "A Special, Olivia Newton-John." Olivia took the American television audience by storm. Her guests included: Lynda Carter as her character of Wonder Woman, Lee Majors as the Six Million Dollar Man, and Rona Barrett. She sang such hits as "If You Love Me," "Have You Never Been Mellow," "I Honestly Love You," and "Let It Shine." The success of this special led to many other appearances on television.

LOVE PERFORMANCE (1976)
Jolene / Take Me Home Country Roads / Let It Shine / Don't Stop Believin' / Let Me Be There / Pony Ride / As Time Goes By/ Maybe I'm In Love With You /

My Love Is Alive / Newborn Babe / Have You Never Been Mellow / If You Love Me (Let Me Know) / I Honestly Love You

ONLY OLIVIA (1977)

Let Me Be There / Have You Never Been Mellow / Take Me Home Country Roads / Pony Ride / Let It Shine / Slow Dancing / My Love Is Alive / Please Mister Please / Maybe I'm In Love With You / As Time Goes By / Sam / Making A Good Thing Better / I Honestly Love You

GREASE (1978)

"This adaptation of the Broadway hit is an exciting, energetic salute to the golden age of rock and roll. Exchange student Olivia Newton-John is "hopelessly devoted" to hip dragster John Travolta. Will she win his heart? Slick as a D.A., and twice as cool."—*BluePrint Magazine.*

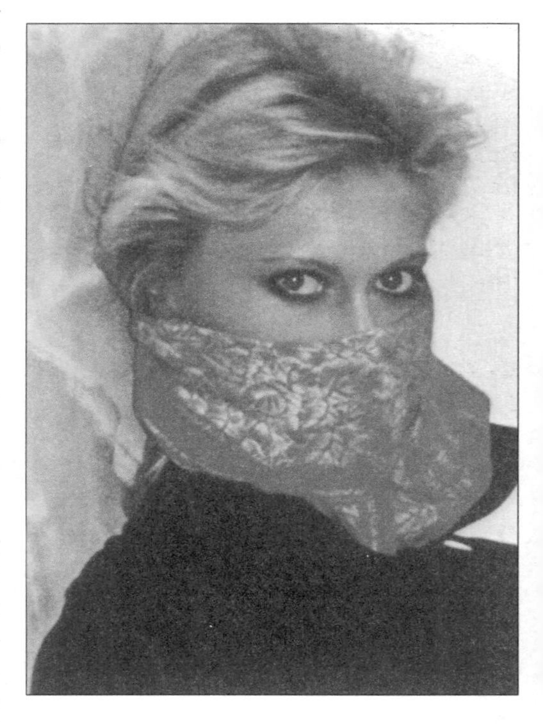

THE BEST OF THE MIDNIGHT SPECIAL (1978)

Olivia performed her latest hit titled "Hopelessly Devoted To You."

XANADU (1980)

Olivia made her first solo starring role in the film *Xanadu.* She starred with Michael Beck and the great Gene Kelly. The story was simple—Olivia was a muse sent from Mt. Helicon to grant two dreams—for Gene Kelly, to get back his big band club, and for Michael Beck, to have success in his life. Olivia and the other eight muses were to make it happen. Of all the places to make it happen, their dreams came together in a disco roller skating rink called Xanadu. The partnership in the movie was successful, the partnership in the theater was not.

THE BEST OF THE MIDNIGHT SPECIAL (1980)

Olivia hosted and performed live tracks from her new movie *Xanadu.* Tracks included: "Magic," "Suddenly" (with Cliff Richard), "Suspended In Time," "Dancin'"(with The Tubes), and "Don't Cry For Me Argentina."

HOLLYWOOD NIGHTS (1980)

"Hollywood Nights," a special shown just before the 1980 Academy Awards, was packed with great entertainment. Performances of "Candle In The Wind" (by Olivia and Elton John), "Suddenly" (by Cliff Richard and Olivia), "I Can't Help It" (by Andy Gibb and Olivia) and "Heartache Tonight" (by Tina Turner, Toni Tenielle, Karen Carpenter, and Olivia), made the night outstanding.

THE BEST OF THE MIDNIGHT SPECIAL (1980)

Olivia hosted and performed live tracks from her hit soundtrack *Xanadu*. Tracks included "Xanadu" and "Magic."

PHYSICAL (1982)

Landslide / Stranger's Touch / Make A Move On Me / Falling / Love Make Me Strong / Physical / Silvery Rain / Carried Away / Recovery / The Promise (The Dolphin Song) / Hopelessly Devoted To You / A Little More Love / I Honestly Love You

OLIVIA IN CONCERT (1982)

Deeper Then The Night / Heart Attack / Magic / Physical / Hopelessly Devoted To You / Make A Move On Me / A Little More Love / Jolene / Silvery Rain / Falling / If You Love Me (Let Me Know) / I Honestly Love You / Please, Mister Please / Sam / You're The One That I Want / Suddenly / Xanadu

TWO OF A KIND (1983)

The movie *Two Of A Kind* flopped at the box office, but the soundtrack skyrocketed and held more top forty hits for Olivia. The premise of the movie was that God was fed up with the way humans were behaving and decided to flood the Earth to get rid of them. At the last minute, four angels—among them Charles Durning, Scatman Crothers, and Beatrice Straight—ask God to spare the Earth. He agrees only if they can show him two selfish people who would sacrifice themselves for each other.

TWIST OF FATE (1984)
With the success of the platinum soundtrack, came the short-form video, "Twist Of Fate." The video included the hits: "Twist Of Fate," "Desperate Times," "Shaking You," "Take A Chance," "Heart Attack," and "Tied Up."

SOUL KISS (1985)
A short-form video of songs from *Soul Kiss* was released. It contained five tracks from the album.

OLIVIA DOWN UNDER (1988)
The album *The Rumour* inspired Olivia to make another long-form video called "Olivia Down Under." It was released on HBO, and then on video. It featured several songs from the album, plus others.

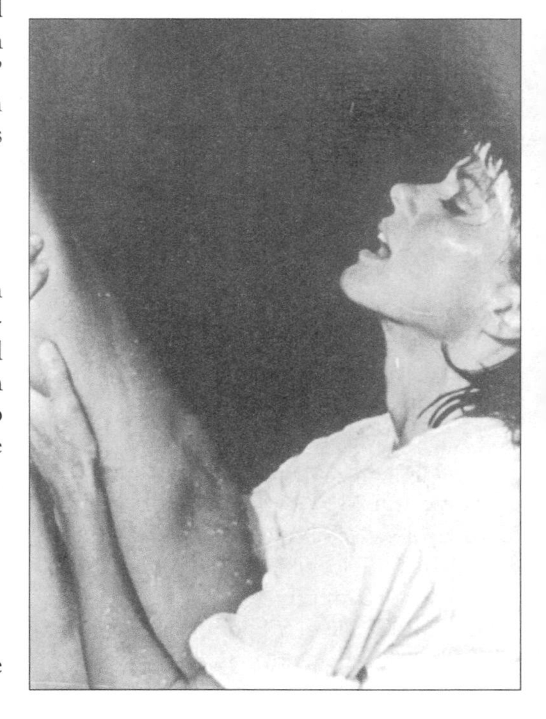

WARM AND TENDER (1989)
VH-1 supported Olivia's album *Warm And Tender* by filming a special of the same name. The special contained interviews, music from the album, a trip to the rainforest to talk about the environment, and the video for "Reach Out For Me."

THE REPORTERS: DESTRUCTION MOTHER EARTH (1989)
Olivia did a segment describing the rainforest devastation.

AN EVENING WITH... FRIEND OF THE ENVIRONMENT (1989)
Featuring live performances from Bette Midler, Cher, Olivia, Goldie Hawn, Meryl Streep, and Robin Williams.

TIMELESS TALES (1989)
Olivia Newton-John makes a chipper hostess for two pleasant half-hour animated tapes from Hanna-Barbera's "Timeless Tales" series. Newton-John introduces the theme: "Even a duck needs a friend, someone to tell him, 'It's okay to be different.'"

Then two real children—gushing such hip words like "Radical!" and "Awesome!"—search an attic for the storybook that come to life.

A MOM FOR CHRISTMAS (1989)

The idea behind the movie, and from the book *A Mom By Magic*, is that a little girl makes a wish in a department store wishing well for a mom for Christmas. Her real mother had died when she was young and she lives with her workaholic father. Just before Christmas, one of the store mannequins (Olivia) comes to life to make the girl's wish come true. As the holiday draws near, the father falls in love with the mannequin; on Christmas, though, the mannequin must return to the store—as she begins to turn back into a mannequin, only the love of the family can bring her back.

IN A NEW LIGHT '92 (1992)

Olivia included herself in the AIDS awareness special "In A New Light '92." In the program, Olivia spoke of her friend Armondo, who died of the disease. She spoke of the pain of not seeing her friend before he died, because she was pregnant, and doctors advised her against it because so little was known at the time. She spoke of the lies she told Armondo—that she was too busy to talk to him or that she was not available. She dedicated her live performance of the song "I Honestly Love You" to his memory.

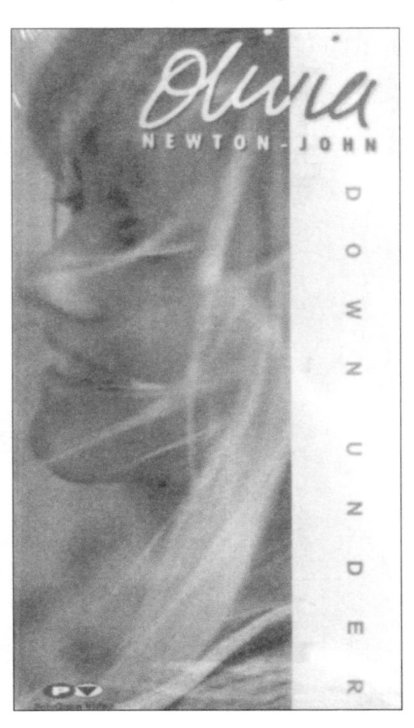

THE WORLD MUSIC AWARDS (1992)

Olivia hosted and performed her latest release "I Need Love," and a duet with Cliff Richard, "Suddenly."

LARRY KING LIVE (1993)

Olivia talked candidly about her life, cancer, her new album and a children's book she had written.

AND THE BEAT GOES ON (1994)

Olivia and other stars from the '70s return for a reunion. She hosted one segment of the show.

SNOWY RIVER: THE MacGREGOR SAGA (1994)

Olivia made a guest appearance in this show which is shot on location in Australia.

Once Upon A Time...
One Little Girl's
Christmas Wish Turned A
Mannequin
Into
A Mom,
And Changed Both
Of Their Lives Forever.
Starring
Olivia Newton-John
In her first made-for-TV movie!
A Mom For Christmas
Also starring
Doug Sheehan
& Doris Roberts
World Premiere Movie!
9PM 10, 12, 29

An evening with...
BETTE midler
CHER
GOLDIE hawn
MERYL streep
OLIVIA newton-joh
& ROBIN willian
...friends of the environment
Join the stars for an evening of music and comedy.
10:00PM

MAGAZINE LISTING

Magazines

PEOPLE
2/75
Olivia Newton-John cover and story

MOVIE WORLD
7/75
Barbra Streisand / Cher cover, Michael Landon, Olivia Newton-John, Robert Redford, Roy Roger, Lucy, Dean Martin

HOLLYWOOD
6/76
Sonny And Cher cover, Oliver Reed, Olivia Newton-John, Dean Martin, Kate Jackson, Penny Marshall, Robert Redford, Lucy

TIGER BEAT
8/76
Olivia Newton-John, Lindsay Wagner, Penny Marshall, David Soul

GOSSIP
12/76
Charlie's Angel, Barbra Streisand, Cher, Kate Jackson, "Starsky and Hutch," Olivia Newton-John, Dustin Hoffman, Kurt Russell

GOSSIP
7/77
Kate Jackson, Lindsay Wagner cover, Lucy, Farrah Fawcett, David Soul, Cher, Richard Chamberlain, Barbra Streisand, Olivia Newton-John, Joi Lansing

TV AND MOVIE SCREEN
7/77
Farrah Fawcett / Marie Osmond cover and illustrated stories, Cher, David Soul, P. M. Glaser, Kate Jackson, Olivia Newton-John

PREVIEW
7/77
Kim Basinger / Kris Kristofferson cover, David Soul, Cher, Barbra Streisand, Kristy McNichol, Olivia Newton-John, Timothy Dalton

LADIES HOME JOURNAL
8/77
Olivia Newton-John cover and story

PREVIEW
9/77
Star Wars cover, Farrah Fawcett, Penny Marshall, Robert Redford, Kim Basinger, Cheryl Ladd, Kristy McNichol, Cher, Cindy Williams, Olivia Newton-John, Wayne Newton, Perry King

MODERN SCREEN
10/77
"Charlie's Angels" cover, Carpenters illustrated story, Cheryl Ladd, Kate Jackson, J.L. Curtis, J. Smith, Olivia Newton-John, Richard Thomas

PREVIEW
12/77
Farrah and Lee Majors cover, Lynda Carter, Tom Jones, Lindsay Wagner, Tom Selleck, Sandy Duncan, Cheryl Ladd, *Grease*

US
1/78
Olivia Newton-John, John Travolta, John Belushi, Jane Curtin, Gilda Radner

PREVIEW SUPER SPECIAL
Spring 1978, #1
Linda Ronstadt / Kris Kristofferson cover, Cheryl Ladd, Lucy, David Soul, Oliver Reed, Farrah Fawcett, Olivia Newton-John, Kate Jackson, Cher, Barbra Streisand, Kristy McNichol

HOLLYWOOD SUPER SPECIAL
Spring 1978
Olivia Newton-John / John Travolta cover, Tommy Lee Jones, Cher, Jerry Lewis, David Soul, Dean Martin, Mike Landon, Joyce Dewitt

US
6/78
John Wayne cover, Olivia Newton-John, Neil Sedaka

PEOPLE
7/78
Olivia Newton John cover and story

PREVIEW
8/78
"Charlie's Angels" cover, Olivia Newton-John, Kristy McNichol, Beatles, Cher, John Belushi

MODERN SCREEN
8/78
Farrah Fawcett / Lee Majors / John Travolta / Burt Reynolds / Olivia Newton-John cover, "Wonder Woman," Osmonds

MOVIE LIFE
9/78
Bee Gees Cover, Olivia Newton-John, John Ritter, Kristy McNichol, Barbra Streisand

US
9/78
Joyce Dewitt cover, Olivia Newton-John, Dyan Cannon, Kiss

GOSSIP
10/78
Olivia Newton-John / John Travolta Cover, Lucy, Farrah Fawcett, Andy & Barry Gibb, Bob Urich, Richard Hatch, Mark Hamill, Cher, Harrison Ford, Penny Marshall

SOUVENIR PROGRAMS
12/78
Mark Hamill / Robin Williams / Jeff Conway cover, Olivia Newton-John, Kate Jackson, Joyce Dewitt

TEEN BEAUTY
#9 , '78
Olivia Newton-John, Kristy McNichol, Wonder Woman, Kate Jackson, Brooke Shields

TIGER BEAT
Super Special #11, '78
Olivia Newton-John, Shawn Cassidy, Osmonds, Joyce Dewitt, Pam Dawber.

US
1978
Olivia Newton-John / John Travolta cover photo and story

US
1978
Olivia Newton-John / John Belushi / Robin Williams cover, Kate Jackson, "Charlie's Angels"

PEOPLE MAGAZINE
3/79
Farrah Fawcett / Kiss / J. Smith, etc. cover & stories, Barbra Streisand, Olivia Newton-John, David Soul, Kristy McNichol, John Belushi, Christopher Reeve, Bee Gees

PREVIEW
4/79
Richard Hatch / Superman / Hulk / Robin Williams cover, Dirk Benedict, Cheryl Ladd, Kate Jackson, Olivia Newton-John, Farrah Fawcett

US
5/79
John Belushi, Dan Aykroyd, Farrah, John Travolta, Cheryl Tiegs, "Mork and Mindy" cover, Olivia Newton-John, Cheryl Ladd

PEOPLE
7/79
Olivia Newton-John cover and story, Roller Mania

WOMAN'S DAY
11/79
Shelley Hack cover & inside, Farrah Fawcett, Cheryl Tiegs, Kristy McNichol, Cheryl Ladd, Olivia Newton-John, Marie Osmond

PREVIEW
11/79
John Schneider / Gil Gerard cover, Robin Williams, Dean Martin, Harrison Ford, Cher, Olivia Newton-John, Ken Wahl, Andy Gibb, Shelley Hack

US
1/80
Star Trek cover, Olivia Newton-John, Mike Beck, Sheena Easton, John Belushi

US
3/80
"Dallas" cover, Olivia Newton-John, Loretta Lynn, John Travolta

HOLLYWOOD
5/80
Mary Tyler Moore / Carol Burnett / Valerie Harper cover, Lucy, Kristy McNichol, Cheryl Ladd, Andy Gibb, Olivia Newton-John

FREE YOU TV MAGAZINE
6/80
Australian: Olivia Newton-John, Andy Gibb, Osmonds, Robert Urich, John Schneider

TEEN BEAT
8/80
John Schneider, Olivia Newton-John, Andy Gibb, Larry Wilcox, Scott Baio, Mark Hamill

US
9/80
Tanya Roberts & five other Angels on cover, Farrah, one-page pull-out, Olivia Newton-John, Mark Hamill, Kristy McNichol, Peter Gunn

MOVIE 80
#4
Olivia Newton-John Cover, Michael Beck, John Belushi, Fame, Kristy McNichol, Angela Lansbury

XANADU
Illustrated Movie Story
#17, '80
Olivia Newton-John / Gene Kelly / Michael Beck cover photo and story

TIGER BEAT
1980
Olivia Newton-John photo story

TEEN TALK
1/81
John Schneider / Olivia Newton-John / Andy Gibb / Mark Hamill cover, Shawn Cassidy

US
3/81
Sally Field cover, Olivia Newton-John, Larry Wilcox, Batman, Cat Woman

US
7/81
Olivia Newton-John cover, Jane Curtin, David Cassidy, Gale Storm

SIXTEEN
10/81
John Schneider cover, Tom Selleck, Olivia Newton-John, Larry Wilcox, Dennis Quaid, Rex Smith

TIGER BEAT STAR
11/81
Olivia Newton-John, Brooke Shields, Mark Hamill, Chris Reeve, REO Speedwagon

SIXTEEN
12/81
John Schneider / Kiss cover, Olivia Newton-John, Andy Gibb, REO Speedwagon, Tom Selleck, Styx

PEOPLE
2/82
Olivia Newton-John cover and story

SIXTEEN
3/82
Olivia Newton-John, Kristy McNichol, John Schneider, Ike Eisenman, Sting, Lorne Greene

SOPHISTICATE'S BEAUTY GUIDE
3/82
Olivia Newton-John, Tom Selleck, Susanne Somers

TIGER BEAT STAR
10/82
Olivia Newton-John, John Schneider, John Stamos, Matt Dillon, Kristy McNichol

US
5/83
Hoffman / Eavens / Selleck cover, Olivia Newton-John, Margot Kidder, Cher, Wonder Woman

CO ED
6/83
Olivia Newton-John cover and story

US
8/83
John Travolta cover story, Olivia Newton-John, Rob Lowe, Elvis

PEOPLE
10/83
Michael Jackson cover story, Olivia Newton-John, Richard Gere, Christopher Walken

US
12/83
007 cover, Olivia Newton-John, Sharon Gless, Tom Selleck, Dan Aykroyd

CINEMA ODYSSEY
Vol. 2, #1, '83
Olivia Newton-John Cover, Tanya Roberts, Mark Hamill, Perry King, *Octopussy*

TEEN BEAT
2/84
Olivia Newton-John, Bruce Penhall, Tom Cruise, Ricky Schroeder, John Stamos, Jon Eric Hexum, Penny Marshall

US
1/85
Olivia Newton-John cover photo and story

SIXTEEN
5/85
John Stamos, Olivia Newton-John, Johnny Depp, Rex Smith, Madonna, John Schneider

ROCK PHOTO
Summer 1985
Madonna cover, Olivia Newton-John, Jennifer Beals

ROCK LINE
8/85
Madonna cover, Olivia Newton-John, Duran Duran, Sting

PEOPLE
9/85
Olivia Newton-John cover and story

WOMAN'S DAY
3/86
Olivia Newton-John cover photo and story, Brooke Shields

US
4/86
Clint Eastwood cover, Olivia Newton-John, C. Thomas Howell

US
5/86
Tony Danza cover, Olivia Newton-John, Martin Sheen, Debra Winger, Debbie Harry

US
6/86
Tom Cruise cover, Olivia Newton-John, Dolly Parton, Dean Martin

PEOPLE
5/87
Madonna / Tony Danza cover story, Olivia Newton-John, Robin Williams

US
6/87
Tom Selleck cover, Olivia Newton-John, Timothy Dalton, Elvira, Mel Gibson

NEW IDEA
7/88
Olivia Newton-John cover & two-color photo story, Patricia O'Neal

PARADE
12/88
Olivia Newton-John article—"In Step With"

TV WEEK
Australia 8/89
Olivia Newton-John cover photo and story, Tom Selleck, Mel Gibson, John Small

TV WEEK
Australia 10/89
Olivia Newton-John, Cher, Madonna, Clint Eastwood, Richard Gere

WOMAN'S DAY
11/89
Olivia Newton-John / Princess Diana cover photo and story, Michael Jackson

US
11/89
Mick Jagger cover story, Olivia Newton-John, Susan Olsen, Clint Black

TV WEEK
Australia 12/89
Olivia Newton-John cover photo and story, Mel Gibson, Robert Englund

US
4/90
Olivia Newton-John inside story

SELF
5/90
Olivia Newton-John inside story

US
9/90
Mel Gibson cover story, Olivia Newton-John, Bryan Adams

CHANNELS
12/90
Olivia Newton-John cover and story—"A Mom For Christmas"

PEOPLE
8/91
Olivia Newton-John cover and inside story

PARADE
5/92
Sean Connery cover, Olivia Newton-John story

CD DISCOVERY
1992
Olivia Newton-John cover and article—"Two Decades Of Hits"

LADIES HOME JOURNAL
6/94
"At Home With Olivia Newton-John"

Promotional picture released by MCA Records

Promotional picture released by Geffen Records